BURLINGTON CENTRAL HIGH SCHOOL
1433 BALDWIN ST.
BURLINGTON, ONTARIO L7S 1K4

HALTON DISTRICT SCHOOL BOARD
BURLINGTON CENTRAL

NAME	CLASS	DATE
Chris Millard	133	Oct 1st
Will Pittmą		
ARNIE	228	Today

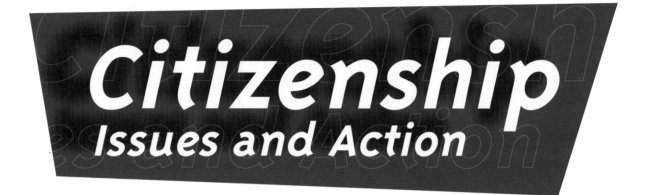

Citizenship
Issues and Action

Mark Evans

Michael Slodovnick

Terezia Zoric

Rosemary Evans

PEARSON

Prentice
Hall

Toronto

Canadian Cataloguing in Publication Data

Main entry under title:
Citizenship : issues and action

For use in grade 10.
Includes index.
ISBN 0-13-088943-1

1. Civics, Canadian. 2. Canada — Politics and government. 3. Citizenship — Canada.
I. Evans, Mark, 1951– .

JL15.C57 2000   320.471   C00-930311-1

ISBN 0-13-088943-1

Publisher: Mark Cobham
Product Manager: Anita Borovilos
Managing Editor: Elynor Kagan
Contributing Editor: Matthew Christison
Lead Developmental Editor: Sarah Swartz
Developmental Editors: Barbara Hehner, Elma Schemenauer
Production Editor: Angelie Kim
Citizenship in Action Profiles: Claudia Bickel
Cover and Interior Design: Alex Li
Page Layout: Anthony Leung
Cover Image: David Oliver/Stone (teenagers), Digital Vision (background)
Illustrations: Teco Guerreiro Rodrigues, Kevin Cheng/Supercat Illustration
Production Coordinator: Zane Kaneps
Photo Research/Permissions: Michaele Sinko, Mary Rose MacLachlan
Literary Permissions: Maria DeCambra

Printed and bound in Canada

8 9 10 FR 10 09 08

Contents

Chapter 3   Participating at the Local Level   70

Chapter 4   Provincial and Federal Governments: Building Your Knowledge   104

Chapter 6   Global Citizenship   178

Preface

Citizenship: Issues and Action provides opportunities for students to explore their role as citizens within a local, national, and global context. Six chapters, ranging from "Me, a Citizen?" to "Global Citizenship," provide opportunities to investigate what it means to be a responsible citizen in a democratic setting. It helps students to understand three important elements that are part of being a citizen in today's world:

- a sense of membership, or identity, with some wider community, such as the local community or nation
- a set of rights and freedoms, such as freedom of thought or the right to vote
- a corresponding set of obligations, such as an obligation to respect the rights of others or a duty to obey the law

While this book introduces the structures, processes, and legal aspects of government institutions, it also allows students to examine the ideas and practices of participating in a democracy. It is issue-based, allowing readers to explore controversies. It will help students develop knowledge and civic literacy skills that they need to take an *informed*, *purposeful*, and *active* role in the civic life of their community.

This book is relevant to real life in the twenty-first century. In each chapter, students are invited to participate actively in questions and issues of civic importance in their own school and community, as well as in the wider world. They are given opportunities to integrate and apply what they have learned in each chapter to authentic decision-making, problem-solving, and conflict-resolution situations. Most important of all, this book will challenge students to think about what citizenship means. Students will be encouraged to get involved, to "make a difference" in all the communities to which they belong — from local to global.

Features of this Book

■ Each chapter begins with an *opening spread* that features a visual and an issue related to a key theme of the chapter. Chapter openers include questions entitled **What Do You Think?**, challenging students to think about the topic before they continue reading the chapter. In the margin, **Focus Your Learning** highlights the curriculum expectations covered in the chapter.

■ Margin notes throughout the chapters include *definitions of key terms* in clear and concise language and **Did You Know?** sections that feature interesting related facts.

■ Every chapter includes 15 or more **Infosources,** documents or illustrations that illuminate the points being made in the text. This *source material* provides added interest, different points of view, and interesting opinions. Special attention is given to stories about youth in action and how young people are making positive contributions to their communities.

■ *Profiles and interviews* with people and organizations relating to the topic appear in special one-page features entitled **Citizenship in Action.** Some of these people are famous and others are people students might meet in everyday life. Some have a long history of civic action; some are still young. All are meant to inspire students as model citizens.

■ *Case studies* appear in sections entitled **Focus on an Issue,** complete with Infosources, illustrations, and questions to guide the investigation. These issues will allow students to explore personal beliefs, values, and the perspectives of others.

■ The many *photographs, cartoons, posters, graphs, charts,* and *timelines* present information in a lively way. They are content-rich, to supplement information in the text.

■ Short *activity blocks* called **The Inquiring Citizen** follow key sections in each chapter. They are divided into three categories for each of the three learning strands: Be Informed, Be Purposeful, Be Active. In these activity blocks, students can check their understanding, analyze what they have read, and research and communicate further ideas, as well as act on them.

- Though practice in literacy and citizenship skills appear throughout the book, each chapter contains one-page sections entitled **Citizen's Toolkit** for selected skills. These are special *skill builders*, especially designed to help students in areas such as writing effectively, detecting bias, and developing a global perspective.

- Each chapter ends with a **Chapter Review.** This section includes questions for review, as well as more extended activities that allow students to put what they have learned into action with simulations, community service opportunities, newspaper development, and other similar activities. Inquiry, critical thinking, decision making, conflict resolution, research, collaboration, and communication are emphasized through a range of engaging independent and collaborative activities.

- Because of the growing importance of understanding and analyzing media and technology, special icons appear to call attention to these areas.

Learning Expectations of this Book

In this book, students are expected to become informed about the principles and practices of democratic decision making. They are asked to investigate beliefs and values that guide purposeful and active citizens in issues of civic importance. They will develop the skills needed to think and act critically and creatively about these matters.

The three central learning strands interwoven throughout the book include:

Informed Citizenship

- principles and practices of democratic decision making
- structures and processes of government decision making
- focus on issues
- rights and responsibilities of citizenship
- contrasting understandings about what it means to be a citizen

Purposeful Citizenship

- beliefs and values underlying democratic citizenship
- exploration of personal beliefs and values, as well as the perspectives of others
- challenges of governing communities in which diverse perspectives exist

Active Citizenship

- inquiry and research skills
- decision making and conflict resolution
- collaboration
- citizenship participation and community involvement

Five key considerations guide the development of the three central learning strands. These include:

- substantive knowledge acquisition
- engaging narrative and interesting authentic sources
- skill building
- beliefs, values, and multiple perspectives
- active involvement

Acknowledgements

We would like to thank Prentice Hall, our publisher, for supporting us, and for believing in the capacity of young people to become informed, purposeful, and active citizens. Thanks to Sarah Swartz, the Project Editor, for her patience, encouragement, cheerfulness, persistence, and fine editing skills; to Elynor Kagan for her dedication to this project and for her willingness to listen and to accommodate our many requests; and to everyone involved with our book, especially Anita Borovilos, Matt Christison, Mark Cobham, Zane Kaneps, Angelie Kim, Anthony Leung, Alex Li, Michaele Sinko, and Barbara Webber. We appreciate your hard work and long hours!

A special thanks to all the community groups, teachers, legislators, administrators, and officials who have supported the work of young people as they gain an understanding of the democratic experience, its opportunities and its challenges.

And most of all, to our families, friends, students, and colleagues, thank you for your understanding, inspiration, and ongoing support throughout the development of this project. Thanks to Paul and Noam; to Pat, Siân, Bryn, Dylan, and Morgan for your encouragement and sense of humour; to Mike, Heather, and Mary for your continuing support and encouragement; and to Thom for your patience and understanding.

We would also like to thank the following people, who have contributed to this text by helping in the development of the manuscript or reviewing the material at various stages.

Joe Cafiso
Joe Capetto
Mike Clare
John Cole
Vince Danetta
Sandy Dobeck
Vern Douglas
John Fiorazanti

Greg Hobbs
Terry Hourigan
Julie Hunt-Gibbons
Jane Isherwood
Tom Kolin
Rick Lund
Bob McGauhey
Reno Melatti

Ross Parkinson
Elena Piezzo
Peter Stefan
Joseph Tersigni
Zubeda Vahed
Allen Vickman
Jodi Zanatta

CHAPTER

1

Me, A Citizen?

FOCUS YOUR LEARNING

The Informed Citizen

What is democratic decision making?

What is a "right"? What is a "responsibility"?

The Purposeful Citizen

How do our beliefs and values affect the way public decisions are made?

How do our beliefs and values affect the way we act as citizens?

The Active Citizen

How can you participate in civic life?

What personal skills and knowledge do you need to become involved in civic life?

Whether or not you know it, you are a citizen in many different ways. For example, you might be a member of the school band or of a neighbourhood lacrosse team. This makes you a citizen of your school and local community. You also have an active role to play as a citizen in your city, province, country, and even in the world at large.

In this book, you will explore what it means to be a citizen. We live in a world that is constantly changing, and as it changes, so does our understanding of citizenship. You will examine what it means to be an active citizen in today's world. You will be encouraged to get involved as a citizen in all the communities to which you belong — from local to global — so that you can shape the future you desire.

Key Terms

- civics
- government
- civil society
- ideology
- democracy
- rights and freedoms
- majority rule
- minority rights
- responsibility
- rule of law

Parents' group argues for tighter censorship rules

EDUCATION shouldn't be a DEBT SENTENCE
Canadian Federation of Students

Ottawa reviews funding for social programs

City studying better wheelchair access in public places

Students volunteer for "Out of the Cold" youth program

STUDENTS MARCH AGAINST VIOLENCE IN SCHOOLS

ONTARIO AND BC REQUIRE CYCLISTS TO WEAR HELMETS

WHAT DO **YOU** THINK?

When you look at headlines like these, you can see that in today's world, we face some difficult issues. Citizenship is about how we choose to respond to these issues. It is about the decisions we make and the actions we take to influence the ways in which our communities change and develop.

Responsible citizenship means having the knowledge to understand the issues we face. It also means using that knowledge to make effective decisions. Are you ready to meet the challenges of the twenty-first century? To what extent will you, as a citizen, participate in shaping your future?

■ From the headlines above, explain some of the challenges we face today. How do these issues affect you as a citizen of your local community? As a citizen of Canada? As a citizen of the world?

■ In small groups, discuss what comes to mind when you hear the word "citizenship." Prepare a word web that reflects your group's ideas. Why might your ideas about citizenship vary?

■ What do you think are the most important characteristics of a responsible citizen?

Why Study Civics?

*Youth must be given a "voice" and role to play in
the making of decisions that affect them.*

— Ontario Coalition for Children and Youth

civics: The study of how
public decisions are made,
of issues that are important
to the public, and of the
rights and responsibilities
of citizens.

As a young citizen of the twenty-first century, you need the right
tools to participate responsibly in society. By studying **civics**, you
will be introduced to the knowledge, skills, and beliefs that will
help you become an informed, purposeful, and active citizen. In
this book, you are invited to:

- find out how our government works and what processes it uses
  to make decisions that affect us all

- identify your personal beliefs and values about how we
  participate in society

- practise basic citizenship skills

- examine the challenges of participating in communities in
  which people often hold differing views

values: Beliefs about what is
most important or valuable in
life.

- think critically about what active and responsible citizenship
  means to you

Once you have a certain amount of
knowledge and some basic skills, you will be
able to participate as a citizen to make a
difference in our society. You will have ideas
about how to act according to your **values** —
your beliefs about what is most important or
valuable. There are many young people, like
you, who contribute to civic life — the life of
their communities.

This student is reading about Rescue Mission: Planet
Earth, an international project on the environment.
Knowledge, skills, and beliefs all play a part in making
us active citizens.

RESCUE MISSION: PLANET EARTH

A group of Canadian students took part in an international project called Rescue Mission: Planet Earth. Together with young people from other countries, they researched environmental issues. They shared their findings in an international teleconference. Their exercise in citizenship did not stop there. The students took what they had learned to their local communities. They spoke about their findings at school board meetings, public functions in their towns, and at their graduation ceremonies. They also met with government representatives to discuss their environmental concerns.

Source: Adapted from www.tgmag.ca/enviro/ag23_e.html

Taking a Stand Against Discrimination

At one Canadian school, students and teachers formed a committee called STAND (Student-Teacher Action for Non-Discrimination). The committee took action against all forms of discrimination that take place in everyday life but go unnoticed. Members organized conferences, held fundraisers, ran letter-writing campaigns, and participated in research on how to oppose discrimination in Canadian society.

Source: Adapted from Winning Ideas to Stop Racism.

ACTIVITIES   THE INQUIRING CITIZEN

BE Informed

1. **a)** Review Infosources 1–1 and 1–2. How did these groups of young people demonstrate citizenship?
   b) What do you think motivated them to get involved? What beliefs and values are shown by their actions?

BE Purposeful

2. Give an example of a time when you or a friend tried to make a difference. What motivated you or your friend to get involved?

3. Look through newspapers and [M] magazines and clip any items related to civic issues. Share your clippings with the class. Discuss what kinds of issues are represented. What sources of information might you use to keep informed about civic life?

BE Active

4. Interview an adult in your family or neighbourhood about a change that has improved your community. Be sure to plan your questions beforehand, and to take notes during the interview. If possible, record the interview. Report to the class on what you have learned.

What Are the Challenges of Living in a Community?

Every day in your life, you have needs and challenges that must be met. You can deal with some of the personal challenges yourself, sometimes with the help of family and friends. Other challenges are more complex and require the help of larger circles of people. Our complex challenges include:

- ensuring that reliable transportation, health care, a police force, firefighters, and many other services are provided in the community
- protecting our rights and freedoms as citizens of a nation, for example, the right to speak openly and the right to choose our friends and associates
- the right to live in a peaceful world without epidemics of disease, famine, or ecological disasters

As a citizen, you are part of many communities, as shown in Infosource 1–3. These communities help you meet your needs in various ways. Many of the challenges we face can be met with the help of support networks — groups of people working together for a purpose. For example, your family and friends help you with many of your needs, such as food, shelter, and affection. More complex challenges require co-operation from a wider circle of people.

Communities have established formal systems and structures to deal with our more complex challenges. These structures are called **governments**. They exist so that we can deal with big challenges that cannot be overcome by individuals or smaller groups. Governments provide us with the formal processes we need to provide major services, to make decisions as a community, and to establish and enforce laws.

Sometimes it can be difficult for a community to satisfy the different needs of all of its members. Because a community is made up of many people, what may be best for you may not always be best for others, or for the community as a whole. Living in a community can sometimes lead to conflict. How can a community protect the rights and freedoms of all its citizens? How can it ensure that citizens live without fear of war or other disasters? How can conflicts be resolved? These are the further challenges of living in a community.

government: A decision-making system that has the power to make laws and direct the affairs of a country, province, or municipality. The word comes from Latin and Greek words that mean "to steer."

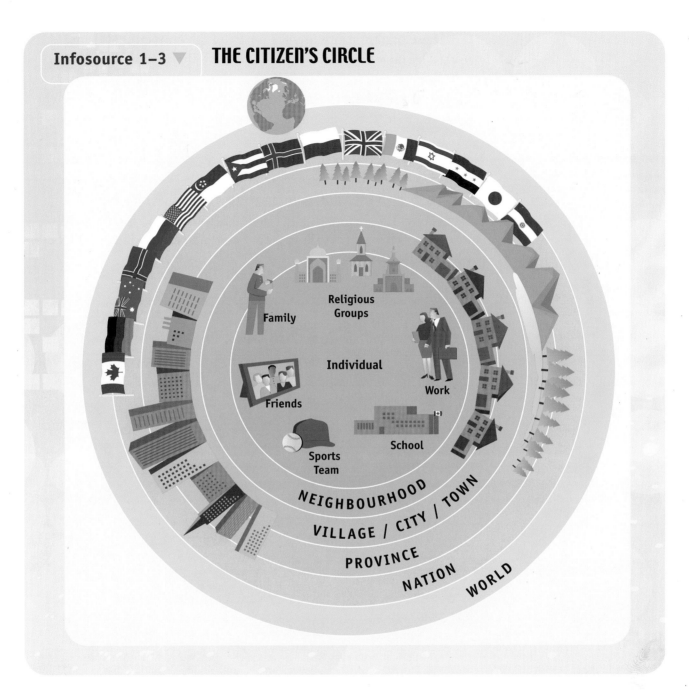

Our Civil Society

Before formal governments existed, humans helped and protected each other. Today, we still help our fellow citizens, often by joining voluntary organizations. There are many organizations that try to make a difference or to meet challenges. They might be concerned with health, youth programs, social services, sports and recreation, arts and culture, religious faith, animal welfare, or international aid.

Did You Know?

There are some 175 000 voluntary organizations in Canada. In Ontario, well over two million people volunteer with these groups.

These organizations are not a part of government. They are started by members who find ways to raise the money they need to run their programs. The members work to provide services and to explain their beliefs to the public, to governments, or to others who might be able to make a difference.

Together, these organizations make up what is known as our **civil society**. Civil society allows groups of people to voice their concerns and to help to solve a variety of problems. Examples of Canadian civil society organizations include the Canadian Environmental Network, the Humane Society, and MediaWatch. International organizations include Greenpeace, Oxfam, and Doctors Without Borders.

civil society: Voluntary organizations of citizens that work to make a difference on important public issues.

Some civil society organizations at work.

Right: Médecins du monde

Bottom left: Greenpeace

Bottom right: Council of Canadians

DOCTORS WITHOUT BORDERS

It's called the Nobel Peace Prize — but the real prize for physicians like Toronto's Dr. Michael Schull is inner peace. Schull signed up with the international volunteer group Médecins Sans Frontières — or Doctors Without Borders — which...won the coveted Nobel Peace Prize. In more than 80 countries, more than 2000 doctors battle daily to save lives in the midst of conflict, waging their own wars against disease and ignorance. But the knowledge that they are making a difference...helps overcome the horrible realities the volunteers are faced with. Doctors Without Borders is an association of people who are deeply committed to providing humanitarian aid in recognition of the basic dignity of human beings. Dr. Schull explains, "It is an organization that will not let borders, laws, or rules stand in the way of basic dignity of people and their right to humanitarian aid."

Source: Adapted from Toronto Star

Dr. Michael Schull

ACTIVITIES   THE INQUIRING CITIZEN

BE Informed

1. With a partner, discuss the following questions:
   a) In your own "Citizen's Circle," which group or community are you most involved with in your day-to-day life?
   b) What personal and community needs does this group or community satisfy?
   c) In your view, what are some of the challenges that come from being part of this group?

2. a) List some of the civil society organizations and government structures that help us to meet our basic needs.
   b) For each one, identify ways in which citizens could get involved in making decisions.

3. For many people, getting involved in a voluntary organization is part of citizenship. In a small group, brainstorm volunteer activities in your school and community. Write a short report on a voluntary organization that interests you. Include the name and address of the organization; its purpose; a contact person; types of activities; requirements for volunteers. Combine your reports in an information booklet on volunteering for use in your school resource centre or local community centre.

Tom Parkinson

Volunteer for "Out of the Cold"
Youth Program

The "Out of the Cold" program provides overnight shelter, food, and warm clothing to young people who live on the streets. It is just one example of our local civil society. Tom Parkinson, age 22, is a volunteer with the program.

Q: Why is it important to have a program specifically for young people?
A: When you're young, there are times when you just want to be around your peers. If you're on the street and your only choice is between staying on the street or going to a shelter that's mostly older people, you might just opt to stay out on the street. When it is strictly for youth, then you might be more open to coming inside, staying and talking.

Q: Are most of the kids who come to the Out of the Cold program homeless?
A: It varies. I've met some kids who don't have any place to stay. They're from other places and they can't make ends meet on their own. Then there are some who need to get away from their families for a time. They need a break from a situation that might be happening at that particular time.

Q: What are your responsibilities as a volunteer?
A: I usually help with setting up and serving meals. Then I sit down and talk, if people want to talk. I get to know people without being intrusive — that's the interaction part. Then it's back to the clean-up, the maintenance, keeping an eye on things.

Q: Have you volunteered anywhere else in the past?
A: I started volunteering with a breakfast program for school-aged children when I was 16. It runs every weekday morning from about 7:00 to 8:30. I've been doing that for the past six years.

Q: Do you think there should be an age requirement for doing volunteer work?
A: No, I think there is always something young people can do to help out. They just need to feel some connection to what they are doing.

Q: How do people find that connection?
A: They have to give it a try. For me, I was surprised at how well I took to volunteer work. It just seemed to feel right, very natural for me. I guess volunteering to me is a form of self expression. I think there are a lot of people who would find volunteer work a good way to express themselves and their beliefs.

Q: What do you enjoy most about volunteering with Out of the Cold?
A: It's very tangible. I do something and I immediately see what happens, what I'm contributing. It makes me feel I can make a difference in my community.

CITIZEN'S TOOLKIT

Reading the Main Idea and Supporting Evidence

Whether you are examining a piece of writing, a video, a cartoon, or another type of source, identifying the main idea and the supporting evidence is a good beginning to obtaining knowledge. The **main idea** is the most important point being stated about the topic, whether it is about a person, place, or thing. **Supporting evidence** is the information that backs up the main point. Learning to locate the main idea and supporting evidence will help you understand and analyze the material you are reading.

To improve your ability to identify the main idea and supporting evidence, follow these steps:

- Concentrate on the main idea — the person, place, or thing — in your source.

- Identify the pieces of information in the source that help describe the main idea.

- Summarize the main idea of the source in your own words, based on the pieces of information that help describe it.

Putting It Into Practice

1. Locate the main idea and the supporting evidence in Infosource 1–4, using the three steps above.

2. Record your conclusions in the following way.

   Main idea:

   Supporting evidence:

   Compare your answer with a partner.

3. As a class, discuss what difficulties you had in distinguishing the main idea from the supporting evidence.

What Are the Challenges of Decision Making?

- School boards should be allowed to decide what students wear to school.
- Local governments should be allowed to make rules about curfews for teenagers.
- Governments should censor music, movies, and videos.
- Corporations should be allowed to advertise in public schools in return for providing schools with sports equipment.

pluralist society: A society in which different groups with a range of beliefs can influence political life.

What is your point of view on the statements above? No matter what your answer, you probably know someone who thinks differently. Canada is a **pluralist society** — one made up of many groups, and in which we accept a range of opinions and values. How can we reach decisions that are fair to all individuals in our pluralist society? How can we even decide who will make these decisions?

A Question of Ideology

People have different views of how decisions should be made and who should make them. Some people believe that humans are naturally good and reasonably intelligent. As a result, they should be free to pursue their personal goals without too many rules. These people suggest that everyone should be involved in decisions of public importance.

Others are more distrustful of human nature. They suggest that people are naturally selfish and greedy, with only a limited ability to make public decisions. Therefore, society requires very clear rules and laws to ensure discipline and stability in the nation. Decisions should be made by one person or by a very small group of people who have a better ability to lead.

ideology: A set of beliefs and values, especially about how society should be organized and what goals it should pursue.

Over time, different ideas about human nature and decision making have been grouped together. These sets of values and beliefs are known as **ideologies**. Ideologies influence the way we think and the way we act as citizens. They also affect how societies are organized and the way decisions are made.

For example, choose one of the statements at the start of the previous page. Now look back at the two groups of people with differing views of human nature. How do you think each group might respond to the statement?

Many different ideologies exist within Canada — and around the world. These different sets of ideas and beliefs often lead to lively debates on civic issues.

Decision-Making Systems

- Who should have authority to make decisions for a society?
- What process should be used to make decisions?
- How should citizens be involved in decision making?

Throughout the world, different groups of people have found different answers to these questions. The methods they use to make decisions reflect their ideologies, as well as various other factors. To understand how decisions might be made in different ways, it is useful to look at two distinct types of decision making: **autocracy** and **democracy**.

In countries that use autocratic decision making, one individual or just a few people make decisions for the rest of the members of their society. Individuals are expected to accept decisions made by the leaders. Their personal freedoms are limited. For example, they might not have the right to criticize their leaders openly. Citizens have very little opportunity to participate in the way public decisions are made. In some situations, leaders use force to control any opposition.

autocracy: A system of government in which a few rulers have power to make decisions for the people.

democracy: A system in which decisions are controlled by the people. The term comes from the Greek words *demo*, meaning "people," and *cracy*, meaning "rule."

Autocratic governments often exist in countries that have been troubled by unrest. Those citizens who support such governments hope that a powerful leader will bring strong and stable government.

The number of countries that are generally described as being democratic jumped from 10 in 1896 to roughly 100 in 2000.

In countries that use democratic decision making, individuals have a say in questions that affect them. They are expected to participate in various ways. They are free to have differing views and goals. Individuals are also expected to act responsibly. This means that each person is expected to make choices, but must accept the consequences of those choices. Each person must also fulfil certain duties.

In reality, there are few countries with decision-making systems that are purely democratic or autocratic. Usually, there are some variations of both forms. In recent years, people in many autocratic countries have challenged their form of government, and more democratic systems have spread. Even so, those democratic systems take many different forms. In Canada, governments make decisions in a manner that respects democratic ideals and principles.

People have fought for democracy, both in countries considered autocratic and those considered democratic. **Left:** Aung San Suu Kyi has spoken out against the autocratic government of Myanmar (Burma). **Right:** Martin Luther King led the fight for civil rights in the United States, a country considered to be democratic.

ACTIVITIES   THE INQUIRING CITIZEN

BE Informed

1. What is an ideology? How can people's views influence their thoughts about how decisions should be made and who should make them?

2. Make a Plus, Minus, Interesting (PMI) chart to compare autocratic and democratic decision making. Which approach is more open to citizen participation? Why?

BE Purposeful

3. **a)** Do you agree or disagree with the statements at the top of page 12? Give reasons for your views.

   b) In a small group, compare your responses. Identify which beliefs and values you share with the group, and which are unique to you. Discuss how your views might influence your ideas about a civic issue.

A Personal Decision-Making Strategy

Think of a difficult personal decision you had to make. How did you weigh the various sides of the issue? Were there other factors that influenced the way you arrived at your decision? What personal beliefs and values influenced the decision that you made? You probably discovered that the process of coming to an important decision is not an easy one.

Consider using the following steps before you make a decision.

Step 1 Define the question, problem, or issue to be decided.

Step 2 Identify your initial choice based on your personal goals and your understanding of the question at hand.

Step 3 Identify other possible options.

Step 4 Explore and gather information about these possible options.

Step 5 Consider the pros and cons of your initial choice and the other possible options according to information available.

Step 6 Choose the best alternative option and state your reasons.

Step 7 Take appropriate action on your choice.

Putting It Into Practice

1. Think of an important personal decision that you have recently made.
    a) How did you make your decision?
    b) What factors influenced — and complicated — your decision?
    c) What was the outcome?

2. Decide on an important decision of interest to you that is about to be made at your school. Using the steps outlined above in the Personal Decision-Making Strategy, decide what your personal choice would be.

3. With a partner, compare your decisions and the steps you went through to arrive at your decision. Discuss as a class what difficulties you encountered in making your personal decision.

What Does Democracy Mean?

The concept of democracy has captured the imagination of people throughout history. It has been put into action in countries around the world. In the process, it has developed many different dimensions. It can mean many things to many people.

Infosource 1–5 ▼

Features of Democracy: A Student Discussion

Linda: I define democracy as a system where everybody's needs and abilities are taken into consideration and where effective debate can occur about public issues.

Tatjana: In a democracy, I have more freedom to say what I think and do what I want, without being afraid that the government will punish me.

Jamal: To be fair, everyone must have equal rights. Democracy means no one gets special treatment.

Fatema: Democracy is about leaders listening to everyone equally and making decisions to benefit the majority of the people.

Jean-Pierre: Democracies must also guarantee that minorities get equal treatment.

Noah: Democracy for me is working within a group of people to make decisions that will benefit as many people as possible.

At one level, democracy is about personal freedom. At another level, democracy is about equality and social justice. Some of the beliefs central to democracy include:

- Citizens should have a voice in decision making.
- All citizens should be treated as equal.
- All citizens should have fundamental rights and freedoms.
- Citizens should have a sense of responsibility to other people in the community.
- Citizens should have a sense of what is socially just.

Origins of Democratic Decision Making

The kind of democratic decision making we practise in Canada is usually traced back to ancient Greece, in the middle of the fifth century BCE. Residents of the independent city states of the time were unhappy that all important decisions were being made by a small group of privileged people. They began to rebel, insisting on being more involved in the decisions that affected their lives.

The leaders of the city states began to listen to the views of citizens on important issues. Eventually, all native-born free men over the age of 18 were allowed to participate in civic affairs. They had the right to vote, hold office, own property, and defend themselves in a court of law. They also had freedom of speech and freedom of assembly. These rights did not extend to women, foreigners, or slaves.

With rights came responsibilities. Citizens of Greek city states were expected to serve in the army, in the navy, and in courts of law. They were also expected to participate directly in the monthly meetings of the governing body, the Assembly. At these meetings, they discussed public issues, decided on questions of public policy, and established laws. Many of the ideas about democracy that were introduced at this time continue today.

Through time, large, modern nation-states replaced the city states. As they did so, democratic decision making evolved throughout the world. Philosophers argued their ideas of what citizenship should mean. Democratic ideals spread. Groups of people in democratic movements all over the world produced documents confirming their rights and freedoms as citizens.

SOME STEPS IN THE TIMELINE OF DEMOCRACY

Below are some of the ideas and events that have contributed to the development of democracy in many forms in different parts of the world. Democracy continues to evolve in different forms around the globe.

c. 1750 BCE

Babylon (an ancient city in Mesopotamia, or present-day Iraq): The Code of King Hammurabi is created, the first known written code for its city members.

508 BCE

Athens: Democracy is established. Citizens are guaranteed the right to membership in the Assembly, freedom of speech, and equality before the law.

c. 400 BCE

India: Public decisions are made by committees of citizens who vote in special assemblies.

1215

England: King John signs the Magna Carta, which states that no one, not even the king, is above the law.

c. 1350

North America: The Iroquois Confederacy of five (later six) nations is founded, practising decision making by consensus (agreement).

1776

United States: Declaration of Independence states that "all men are created equal" and that governments derive "their just powers from the consent of the governed."

1789–1794

France: The French Revolution ends absolute monarchy (complete control by the king) and introduces Declaration of the Rights of Man, emphasizing liberty, equality, and fraternity.

1919

India: Mahatma Gandhi begins passive resistance campaign to win India's independence from Britain.

1948

The United Nations issues the Universal Declaration of Human Rights, defining basic rights that all people should have.

1982

Canada: Charter of Rights and Freedoms is added to Canada's Constitution.

1990s

Pacific Asia: Asian-style democracies established in many countries in the area.

1994

South Africa: Democracy is established after a long fight against Apartheid, a policy that prevented Black citizens from voting.

Democracy Today

For much of human history, people were considered "subjects" of a ruler, rather than "citizens" of a country. In modern society, respect for citizens and their rights is considered the most important foundation for a democratic nation.

As you have seen, there are more countries with a democratic system of government than ever before. Some countries have been democracies for over a hundred years. Other democracies are new and fragile. Many societies in the world today are undergoing massive changes. Some countries that once provided security, stability, and order — whether democratic or autocratic — are now facing less certain futures. In the democratic world, it is up to citizens to chart a course for the future.

ACTIVITIES　THE INQUIRING CITIZEN

BE Informed

1. a) Examine the views on democracy given in Infosource 1–5. Summarize the ideas about democracy and democratic decision making suggested in the dialogue.
   b) With whose view do you agree the most? Why?

2. When you and your friends are planning to do something together, do you make decisions in the way that Linda suggests in Infosource 1–5? Provide an example to support your answer.

3. Identify three decisions that were made in a group or association to which you belong. Consider clubs, teams, classes, and other social organizations. For each decision, explain:
   a) how the decision was made
   b) how you were involved in the decision-making process
   c) to what extent the process was democratic

4. a) What does it mean when people say that democracy in Greek city states was "by the people"? Who was excluded from the definition of "people"?
   b) How has our understanding of "by the people" changed?

BE Active

5. Research one event shown in Infosource 1–6. Alternatively, select another event in a country of your choice that illustrates the development of a democratic system. In the role of a news reporter at that time, write a brief article that describes the event and its significance. Answer the questions Who? What? When? Where? Why? and With what consequences?

What Are Our Rights?

As democracy has evolved, so have our ideas of what rights citizens should have. Today, democracies recognize a wide variety of rights — civil, political, and social.

Infosource 1–7 ▼

Our Rights: Changing Ideas

Civil Rights	Political Rights	Social Rights
Emphasized in the 18th century. Included:	Emphasized in the 19th century. Included:	Emphasized in the 20th century. Included:
• equality before the law • liberty of person • freedom of speech, thought, and religion • right to own property	• right to participate in elections • right to run for and hold office • right to vote	• right to a certain standard of economic and social well-being • right to participate fully in society

rights and freedoms: Those things we are morally or legally entitled to have or to do.

Today, our fundamental rights are sometimes described in terms of "freedom from" and "freedom to." As a result, they are known as our **rights and freedoms**. Rights and freedoms refer to all of those things that we are morally or legally entitled to have or to do.

In Canada, you have certain fundamental rights and freedoms within your own country, guaranteed by the Canadian Charter of Rights and Freedoms. You will learn more about the Charter in Chapter 2. You also have rights that are upheld by international documents, such as the Universal Declaration of Human Rights and the United Nations Convention on the Rights of the Child. You will learn more about these documents in Chapter 6.

DEMOCRATIC RIGHTS

Freedom from...

All people have the right to protection *from* obvious forms of injustice, such as violence, exploitation, abuse, and torture. They also have a right to have their basic survival needs met, to be free from the more subtle injustices of poverty, hunger, lack of health care, and environmental pollution.

Freedom to...

Everyone has the right *to* participate in those human activities that allow one to develop fully, such as education, the practice of one's religion, culture, and language, the freedom to express opinions, to be part of associations, and to have access to information.

Source: Education for Development, UNICEF

THE RIGHT TO PARTICIPATE

When I look at the struggles of the women's movement for women's equality, for me that's essentially a fight for democracy. When I look at anti-racist struggles, for me these are fights for democracy. When we have labour fighting for the rights of workers to have control over their work environment or over what they produce, for me that's democracy: a fight to make democracy real in people's lives.

Sunera Thobani, former president of the National Action Committee on the Status of Women (NAC)

Source: Our Times

What rights and freedoms are citizens exercising here?

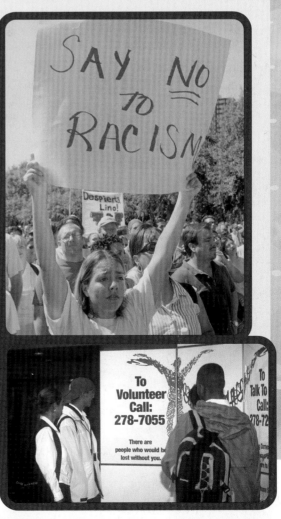

MediaWatch

Responding to the Media

In Canada, we have the freedom to express opinions. Often, opinions are expressed through the media. Television, radio, movies, music videos, advertising, and the Internet all offer powerful ways of communicating differing views. This means that the media express a range of opinions. It also means that the media are likely to present opinions that are not always acceptable to all Canadians.

MediaWatch is an organization that monitors the media. In particular, its members are concerned with the way women are presented. The organization believes that the media often show women in negative ways. Images of women are often provocative, and models are unrealistically slim or glamorous. In some cases, music videos or Web sites suggest violence towards women. MediaWatch argues that this type of treatment has a negative impact on women in real life.

A volunteer organization, MediaWatch was founded in 1981. Since then, it has worked to encourage the media to portray women and girls positively and realistically. One of its aims was to pressure government to make rules about the treatment of women in the media. In 1986, the CRTC (Canadian Radio-television and Telecommunications Commission) decided that all radio and television stations in Canada must follow certain guidelines on how they represent women. Since then, MediaWatch has continued with a variety of campaigns.

Citizens who have a complaint about something they have seen in the media can contact MediaWatch. The organization will advise them on how to make their objections heard—for example, by explaining what kind of letter to write, and to whom the letter should be sent. Sometimes MediaWatch will aim to educate the public on a particular issue. In one case, for instance, it raised public support for removing a sexist beer commercial from public transit vehicles. After the commercial was taken down, MediaWatch members worked with the transit authority to draw up guidelines for ads it would allow on its property in the future.

MediaWatch volunteers also give workshops in schools, where students are encouraged to think critically about what they see in the media. They are asked to think about the impact of media messages on the way they think about themselves and about others. MediaWatch also keeps the public updated on media issues through its Web site at www.mediawatch.ca.

Who Are the People?

Democracy presumes that power rests ultimately with the people.
It is about people feeling that their voice makes a difference.

— Maude Barlow and Bruce Campbell

Ancient Athens called itself a democracy because all citizens could take part in political decisions. But "all citizens" did not mean "all adults" and it definitely did not mean "all young people." As noted, women, slaves, and residents from other Greek cities had no right to participate in government decisions. Young people were not allowed to participate either. In most early democracies, the rights of citizenship were limited, usually to adult men.

As time passed, however, expectations changed. Today, the rights of citizenship have been extended to a much greater number of people in democratic countries. When we say that, in a democracy, "the people decide," we assume that decisions are made by the majority of people. Nevertheless, many questions remain: How should decisions be made when different perspectives exist about a public issue? How do we ensure that the rights of minorities are respected?

Majority Rule versus Minority Rights

Many democracies rely on a simple majority (that is, 50 per cent plus one) to make decisions when different opinions about a public issue exist. This is considered fair, and the majority is thought more likely to have the correct opinion than the minority. **Majority rule** means that the majority is entitled to have its way, even if the minority disagrees. Yet we also believe that all citizens have equal rights. How, then, can we ensure that the majority doesn't deny the rights of the minority? How can **minority rights** be protected, if the needs or wishes of the minority clash with those of the majority?

This has always been one of the most difficult issues of democracy. As far back as the early 1800s, a French scholar named Alexis de Tocqueville travelled in the United States. Based on the new forms of democracy he saw there, he warned against "the tyranny of the majority." His solution was that a democratic government must do what it can to protect and respect the rights of minority groups. Over 150 years later, Nelson Mandela, president of South Africa, made a similar point: "Democracy is based on the majority principle.

majority rule: The principle that the opinion of the greater number should prevail.

minority rights: The principle that the rights of the minority must be safeguarded.

At the same time, democracy also requires that the rights of political and other minorities be safeguarded."

As a result, documents such as the Canadian Charter of Rights and Freedoms and the Universal Declaration of Human Rights do more than lay out rights for the majority. They recognize the rights of all groups. In addition, minority rights are protected to some extent by the responsibilities that all citizens have, as you will see in the section on "What Are Our Responsibilities?" (page 26).

Consensus Decision Making

consensus: A collective decision to which all parties agree.

Not all democratic societies use majority rule to make decisions. Some societies make decisions by **consensus**, or collective agreement. The goal of consensus decision making is to reach a conclusion with which all members of the group can agree. This does not mean that all members are completely satisfied by the final outcome. However, it does mean that everyone involved in making the decision finds it acceptable.

Infosource 1–10 ▼

TRADITIONAL IROQUOIS DECISION MAKING

In about the year 1350, five Iroquois nations formed a union or confederacy. Later, this union became the Six Nations, with the addition of the Tuscarora tribe around 1722. The nations pledged to support each other and to live together in peace. It was agreed that each nation should handle its own internal affairs. For example, a problem affecting only Mohawks would be resolved within the Mohawk longhouses, or decision-making bodies. However, matters of mutual concern to members of the confederacy were addressed collectively. These issues were discussed at meetings in the main longhouse, or council house. Each nation was represented by a number of chiefs, with a total of 50 attending meetings around the council fire. Each chief was free to express the opinions of his nation.

Before a question was discussed in council, the chiefs of each nation got together and agreed among themselves on the issue at hand. In the council, the chiefs then spoke for their particular nation as one unit, trying to persuade the chiefs of the other nations that their ideas were the best. The discussion would go on in council until all five sets of chiefs reached agreement. The confederacy could not take action until there was unanimous agreement among all the nations.

Source: Six Nations Reserve

This photo was taken in about 1910, in the council house in Ohsweken, Ontario. The Iroquois Confederacy Council continued to make decisions on the Six Nations Reserve until 1924, when it was replaced by an elected council.

ACTIVITIES — THE INQUIRING CITIZEN

BE Informed

1. **a)** Review Infosource 1–8. Which three freedoms do you believe are most important? Give reasons for your choices.
   b) Compare your choices with a partner's. In what ways are they similar or different? What do you think accounts for their similarities or differences?

2. **a)** Explain how the photographs in Infosource 1–9 illustrate "freedom from" or "freedom to."
   M b) Using newspapers and magazines, find three additional photographs that show examples of "freedom from" or "freedom to."

3. **a)** In your own words, explain what is meant by "majority rule."
   b) Do you think majority rule is a fair way to make decisions? Explain.

BE Purposeful

4. **a)** What is MediaWatch, and what is its purpose?
   b) What methods does MediaWatch use to reach its goals?
   c) How much influence do you think organizations like MediaWatch should have on the people who make decisions about what we watch and listen to? Give reasons for your view.

5. Describe the main features of consensus decision making, as described in Infosource 1–10. What values are evident in consensus decision making? What do you see as the strengths and weaknesses of this method?

BE Active

6. Research an incident when young people's rights have been upheld or denied, either in your community or elsewhere. Prepare a comic strip illustrating the incident. Write a brief description of events on the back of the comic strip.

What Are Our Responsibilities?

While citizens have rights, they also have **responsibilities**. Often the two are directly linked. For example, if we have the right to drive a car, we also have the responsibility to drive safely and obey traffic laws. If we have the right to vote, we also have the responsibility to use our vote to express our opinions in elections. With the privilege of free medical care and subsidized education that we enjoy as Canadians comes the duty to pay taxes. Just as we are promised equality, so we are obliged to avoid discrimination against others.

Some of these responsibilities are drawn up in laws that can be enforced. Others are based on morality and social conscience — that is, on what we believe to be right and fair. And some are general responsibilities that include:

- becoming informed about the issues that our society faces
- listening to the ideas of others and respecting their rights
- using our skills and abilities in a socially useful manner
- being actively and thoughtfully involved in protecting our own and other people's rights
- participating in improving our communities, if we disagree with certain decisions and laws as they exist

These rollerbladers have the responsibility to skate within the maximum speed limit, for their own safety, as well as the safety of others. Local police have set up radar guns along this stretch of Vancouver's Stanley Park to crack down on speeding rollerbladers.

The Rule of Law

Let's look at responsibilities that are based in law. Democracies are governed by the **rule of law**. This means that there are laws that apply to everyone equally, including those in positions of power. The rule of law protects people from the changing whims of their rulers or leaders. In other words, the rule of law protects the rights of all citizens.

At the same time, every citizen has the responsibility to obey the laws of the land. Laws carry consequences, including penalties, if they are disobeyed. For instance, speed limits on highways and roads are enforced by law, and speeders are fined if they are caught. There are other legal responsibilities. Every Canadian citizen, for example, has a legal responsibility to serve on juries when asked, to pay taxes, and to assist police in maintaining order.

rule of law: The principle that people are governed by laws and that no person is above the law.

Common Goals

One of our responsibilities as citizens is to contribute to the common goals of our community, so that the community, as a whole, will benefit. It can be difficult to decide what these common goals should be or how they should be achieved. However, there is general agreement that we should try to meet certain basic human needs for all people. These needs include adequate housing, proper nutrition, and medical treatment. Beyond these basic needs, common goals might include a reduced crime rate, a better education system, increased trade with other nations, and many other possibilities.

What is the role of police services?

Do these restrictions promote common goals? Explain.

NO LOITERING . NO SOLICITING

Common goals often serve as a guide when communities make decisions or take certain actions. For example, a community might decide that there is a need to reduce violence. Members of the community will then take various actions to accomplish the goals. The actions might be carried out by support networks, civil society groups, or government agencies. Individuals will also support these goals, through local organizations or through the political process.

Personal interests and the goals and interests of the larger community sometimes conflict. Take, for example, the signs shown in the margin. In situations like these, it is sometimes difficult to ensure that decisions are made not only "by the people," but also "for the people." In other words, some decisions may not be popular, but most citizens are ready to abide by them because they are made for the common good.

ACTIVITIES · THE INQUIRING CITIZEN

BE Informed

1. a) Review the responsibilities listed on page 26. Which do you practise most often? Least often?
   b) How would you define a responsible citizen?

2. In what ways does the rule of law affect your day-to-day responsibilities? What would happen if you did not fulfil these responsibilities?

BE Purposeful

3. Car emission tests, anti-smoking laws, and seat belt laws are examples of our efforts to serve common goals. In these examples, how do common goals conflict with individual rights? How do you think these conflicts should be resolved?

BE Active

4. Collect stories from newspapers or magazines about students who have acted responsibly or irresponsibly. Analyze one article for the following information:
   a) In what way was the young person responsible or irresponsible?
   b) Did this person's action help or hurt others? How?
   c) What can be learned from this story?
   d) Report your findings to the class. Begin a bulletin board display that shows ways in which young people contribute to their communities.

FOCUS ON AN ISSUE

Do Schools Balance the Rights and Responsibilities of Students?

In Canada, you are considered a child until you reach the age of 18. This means that you do not have all of the same rights and responsibilities as adults. For example, you are unable to vote until you are 18. At the same time, your rights as a young person are specifically covered by certain laws. One of these laws is the Education Act, which sets out some of the rules that apply to you while you are at school.

Take the following quiz to see how much you know about your rights and responsibilities at school.

Infosource 1–11 ▼ **Rights and Responsibilities Quiz**

True or False:

1. The police can arrest you for skipping school.
2. You do not have to go to school if your parents are teaching you at home.
3. Your principal cannot suspend you just because you swear in class.
4. No one is allowed to go through your personal things at home or in your locker.
5. You can be punished for expressing your opinions in class if they are not what your teacher believes.
6. Your teacher is allowed to hit you.
7. You can protest without fear of being punished if you feel your school is treating you unfairly.

Source: Adapted from www.hri.ca/children/youth

Answers:

1. **True.** Truancy is a crime.
2. **True.** If you are receiving "satisfactory instruction" at home, you do not have to go to school.
3. **False.** You can be suspended for using "profane and improper" language.
4. **True.** Technically, you are protected against "unreasonable search and seizure." What "unreasonable" means, however, is debatable.
5. **False.** Technically, everyone has the freedom of thought, belief, opinion, and expression, although limits may be placed on this freedom.
6. **True.** Teachers are given the same power as parents, which includes using force by way of correction, as long as the force is not unreasonable under the circumstances. Many school boards, however, will not allow teachers to use this power.
7. **True**, but with limits. As a Canadian citizen, you have the freedom of peaceful assembly, but a variety of laws and rules might limit this freedom.

If you look at the answers to the quiz, you will see that there are specific laws meant to protect young people. But are these laws always in the best interests of society? Do they allow young people to ignore their responsibilities and escape the consequences of their actions? People have different responses. Read the following case report and see what you think of the decision made by the court.

Infosource 1–12 ▼

The Case of Regina v. H.

One day a 13-year-old student, called H., and some friends took money from a teacher's purse at school. When the teacher discovered the theft, she reported it to the principal. Later, the teacher told her students about the theft. She said that if the money were returned to her, nothing more would happen. As a result, H. and the others came forward and confessed to the theft.

The teacher didn't inform the principal of her promise. When the school principal found out who had taken the money, he demanded that H. and the others who had participated attend a meeting in his office. There the youths again spoke openly about their involvement in the theft. Throughout the entire discussion in the principal's office, H. was never advised of his rights. As a young person, he had the right to have an adult or lawyer present while being questioned about the theft. Instead, the principal called the police and the youths were all charged with theft.

Later, the youths were acquitted by a judge after he ruled that H. had been denied his rights. As a result, his confessions were inadmissible (not allowed to be considered by the court).

Source: Adapted from Alberta Law Reports

ANALYZING THE ISSUE

BE Informed

1. **a)** Review the questions and answers to the quiz. Which items point out rights of students and which point out responsibilities?
   b) Did any of the answers surprise you? Explain.

2. In the case of Regina v. H., why was H. acquitted? Support your answer with details from Infosources 1–11 and 1–12.

BE Purposeful

3. Why do you think young people have the right for an adult to be present when they are being questioned about a crime?

4. Review your school's current Code of Conduct.
   a) What are your rights under the Code?
   b) What are your responsibilities?
   c) Do you think there is a fair balance between rights and responsibilities?

How Can Citizens Participate in Decision Making?

When a man takes no interest in public affairs,
we think of him not as a man who minds his own business,
but as one who is good for nothing.

— *Athenian philosopher Pericles, fourth century* BCE

If a society is to be democratic, its citizens must participate to influence decisions that will affect their lives. Being involved in your community brings many benefits. You can communicate your ideas and concerns on public issues, and help to shape aspects of life that affect you. At the same time, you will probably find that participating helps you to feel good about yourself, because you are making a difference. It can also broaden your network of friends!

In a democratic society, people participate in many different ways. Voting is the most common form of participation. Working with a political party, or helping out at election time, is also a possibility. Many people also choose to be involved in civil society groups, as you have seen. Other people prefer a more direct approach. They contact government representatives to voice their opinions on public issues. Some express their views in more dramatic ways, perhaps in public demonstrations or marches. All of these forms of participation are part of our democratic heritage.

What are the different forms of participation shown here?

Can Young Canadians Make a Difference?

There are many different ways for young people, like you, to participate. As you saw in Infosource 1–1 and 1–2, you can get involved in a cause you believe in. You can join a political party or shovel snow for a housebound neighbour. You can volunteer to help at a food bank or tutor a child. Young Canadians have participated in such projects as cleaning up local parks and rivers, improving the food on the menu at their school's cafeteria, and establishing peacemaking programs in their schools. If you find out about an issue that concerns you, you can act. Many young people become involved in issues that they observe in their everyday lives.

Infosource 1–13 ▼

SOME TEENS WHO HAVE MADE A DIFFERENCE

Mary Beth developed a theatre program to make fellow students aware of the problem of violence against women. Her group presented skits that rotated around the school during lunch hour, contrasting scenes of violence and harmony.

Andreea gathered support for a teen peer counselling program. She wrote a proposal for funding the project and gathered media support.

Lai Har led student opposition to a transit fare hike. He produced posters and flyers to educate the public and politicians on the effect fare increases would have on students.

Bob was part of an environmental club that helped low-income residents in their community insulate their homes with weather stripping, caulking, and plastic storm windows, to save energy and costs.

Source: Adapted from The Future Is Ours

Although you can participate in a number of ways, it can be harder for young people to have an impact on official decisions. Nevertheless, it is important to remember that the effort is worthwhile, even if you are not completely successful. It is your right and responsibility to become involved in community issues.

Sometimes the actions of young people really do pay off. Infosource 1–14 describes one such case. A group of students convinced a city council to lower the speed limit on the road outside their school.

Infosource 1–14 ▼

Class Fights City Hall on Speed Limit — and Wins

A grade 8 class has made civic history by being the first group ever to persuade a city committee to lower the speed limit on one of its roads. "People underestimate what children can do," said Grace Kim, 13, who helped persuade the planning and transportation committee to cut the 50 km/h speed limit. "It's a rare thing that politicians ever change their minds. They don't usually listen to what students say," she said. Grace and the rest of her grade 8 class also won a recommendation to build a $20 000 crash guard between the south-western portion of the four-lane roadway and the sidewalk to protect students walking to and from their school....

Aware that they faced a tough audience with city politicians, the students did plenty of homework before making their pitch. They arrived on the morning of their presentation with graphs, charts, and a slide show professional enough to compete with many presentations made by the seasoned lobbyists who frequent the city's committee rooms....

Source: Adapted from Toronto Star

Cindy Keiu, Grace Kim, and Cindy Hau fought to lower the speed limit on this road, and won.

The grade 8 students chose a range of actions that helped them to succeed. There are other forms of action that have been used by other groups at other times. Infosource 1–15 lists some of them.

Infosource 1–15 ▼

Some Ways of Taking Action

Protest and Cooperation

- Write letters to the editor or to government representatives.

- Hold public meetings and sign petitions.

- Advertise your cause with flyers, posters, and newsletters.

Non-Cooperation

- Refuse to buy from a certain place or country.

- Refuse to obey a law that you think is unjust.

- Refuse to pay some or all of your taxes.

Intervention

- Participate in demonstrations.

- Put yourself between people or groups trying to harm others.

- Occupy land that is being misused.

Source: Adapted from Biting the Moral Bullet

ANALYZING THE ISSUE

BE Informed

1. Review Infosources 1–13 and 1–14. Choose one example.
   a) How would the community benefit from the action described?
   b) How do you think the action described would affect the student(s) personally?

2. Look at Infosource 1–15. Which of these strategies might have been used in the example you chose above?

3. **a)** Are there any actions in Infosource 1–15 that you personally might take? Explain.
   b) Are there any that you probably would not take? Explain.

BE Active

4. **a)** In a group, select a change you would like to see made in your school. Devise a strategy that you think would bring about the change. Then discuss what obstacles you might encounter.
   b) As a class, discuss: Do you think teenagers like yourself can really make a difference?

ᴮᴱ Informed

1. Use each of the terms below in a sentence, taking care to show how the term is connected to what it means to be a citizen:
   a) right
   b) responsibility
   c) civil society
   d) autocracy
   e) majority rule
   f) minority rights
   g) rule of law

2. a) Work in a group to review what it means to be a citizen. Revise your Citizenship word web (see page 3) to include ideas you have gathered from this chapter.
   b) Create a collage that illustrates five essential qualities of a good citizen, based on information in your word web.

ᴮᴱ Purposeful

3. a) Visit the Youth in Action Network (http://www.mightymedia.com/act) to find out what young people around the world are doing to bring about change in their schools and communities, as well as nationally and internationally.
   b) Profile one Youth in Action project that interests you. Identify the name of the project, its purpose, what volunteers do, its successes, and its future plans.

4. a) Working in a small group, prepare a list of rules for an ideal school, in which everyone is treated fairly and equally. Include rules that prohibit certain types of action as well as rules that encourage certain types of behaviour. Keep in mind the following possibilities:
   - a rule that will allow all students to feel safe from all kinds of dangers
   - a rule that will allow all students to feel that they are respected
   - a rule that will allow all students to have an equal chance to take part in everything that goes on in the school
   - a rule that will allow all students to have similar materials and resources
   - a rule that will allow all students to have an equal chance to learn and succeed

   b) Present your rules to the class, and post them on the board.
   c) As a class, identify the rights that have been listed. Then identify the responsibilities. What are the values that have influenced your class's view of what is fair?
   d) You might want to inform other people about your ideas for rules to ensure fair and equal treatment for all students. Write a letter to your principal, write an article for the school newspaper, or make a presentation at a student council meeting.

Source: Adapted from Education for Development

ᴮᴱ Active

5. a) Prepare a proposal that outlines a process for your school for making important decisions that affect the students. Make sure your proposal includes:
   - a statement of beliefs about whether or not students should be involved in the decision-making process
   - a method for determining which issues or problems should be dealt with
   - a method for identifying and assessing possible solutions
   - an example of how this decision-making process might work with an issue that is important to students in your school at present
   - a summary of how the method you propose is different from methods of decision-making currently used at your school

   b) Submit your proposal to your school's student council and/or teacher council. Consult with your teacher, other students, and members of each council to ensure that your ideas are clear, convincing, and informed.

2 Introducing Our Canadian Government

Is Canada the best country in the world in which to live? The United Nations thinks so. For several years in a row, the UN ranked Canada number one among nations in quality of life. Yet Canada is not an easy country to govern. It is a vast nation with a rich history of conflict and compromise. Canadian citizens vary in race, religion, language, economic status, cultural traditions, experiences, values, and beliefs. This diversity brings many benefits, but it also brings challenges.

In this chapter, you will explore how our democratic system allows for such diversity. You will look at some important features of our system of government and will examine some of the forces that influence our political system. You will also make some decisions about your own role as a citizen in a democracy.

Key Terms

- constitution
- federal system of government
- jurisdiction
- constitutional monarchy
- direct democracy
- representative democracy
- referendum
- franchise
- social movement

WHAT DO **YOU** THINK?

Most people think of Canada as a country with a democratic government. For instance, Canadians enjoy civil rights, such as the freedom of speech, and political rights, such as the right to vote in elections. Yet there are times when some Canadians feel that their government is not responding to their needs or wishes. Opinions often clash in a huge country with such a diverse population. Governments might find it difficult to address the needs of varied regions, groups, and individuals.

- In which ways is Canada a diverse country?

- How does this diversity make governing the country a difficult task?

- Think of a time when you felt that government was not responding to your needs, or to the needs of other groups you are aware of.

- Suggest some steps that could be taken to make government more aware of your concerns.

Why Do Canadians Need Government?

Canada is made up of over 29 million citizens. Each citizen has unique hopes, desires, goals, and ideas about the type of society in which he or she wants to live. As a society, Canadians require a way to make decisions to achieve common goals. Therefore, Canada, like all other nations, has established a system of government to deal with important issues that affect its citizens. Our government exists so that Canadians can accomplish what they want or need, but cannot accomplish as individuals.

GOVERNMENT IN ACTION

What examples of government activity can you identify in these photos? Why would it be difficult for individuals to handle these actions for themselves?

FACTORS SHAPING HOW CANADA IS GOVERNED

A Diverse Cultural History

- Canada's first self-governing nations were the Aboriginal peoples. Today, Aboriginal peoples are working to re-establish a system of self-government.

- The French were the first European settlers. They brought a new system of written laws and political ideas.

- British settlers brought their own political system, which has had an important influence on Canada.

- Waves of immigration, especially in the later part of the twentieth century, have reshaped Canada's political community.

Economics

- Governments play a role in the economy. For example, they run our education and health care systems, provide consumer protection laws, and regulate some business activities.

- Canada faces some economic challenges. For example, there is a significant gap between those who are rich and those who are poor.

Technology and Industry

- Canada is an industrialized and technologically developed country. This creates opportunities, such as the economic resources that governments require to run social programs. It also creates challenges, such as environmental problems.

Geography

- Canada is a huge country with many regions. People in each region tend to face different issues and sometimes want different things from the government.

Global Forces

- The influence of world events and decisions made on the global stage on Canadian life is strong and getting stronger.

- The influence of our neighbour, the United States, is particularly strong.

Values, Beliefs, and Ideologies

- Canadians share many common values, yet they also disagree on some social, political, and economic issues. Governments must take these values, beliefs, and ideologies into account.

What Is Canada's Constitution?

constitution: The supreme law of the land. It outlines the government structure for a nation, and defines and limits government power.

John A. Macdonald and the other representatives who wrote the original constitution are called the Fathers of Confederation. Because there were different representatives at three different conferences held in Charlottetown (1864), Quebec (1864), and London (1866–67), it is unclear exactly who is included in this group.

A **constitution** is the supreme law of the land. It provides a "blueprint" or framework that accomplishes two important tasks. First, it outlines the structure for governing a nation. Second, it defines and limits which government authorities have what power.

In Canada, our constitution has two parts: the written constitution and the unwritten constitution. The first part of Canada's constitution was called the British North America Act (BNA Act). It was written in 1867 by John A. Macdonald and other political representatives from Ontario, Quebec, and the Maritimes during Confederation — the creation of Canada. Because Canada was a colony of Great Britain, the constitution was then passed by the British Parliament. The BNA Act stated that Canada's constitution was to be "similar in principle to that of the United Kingdom." It also:

- created and described Canada's system of government
- stated how powers would be divided among the monarch, the federal Parliament, and the provincial legislatures

Over the years, the original constitution had a number of amendments (changes) added and became known, all together, as

the Constitution Acts, 1867–1982. Until 1982, any changes to Canada's constitution had to be approved by the British Parliament. In 1982, our constitution was patriated (brought home). This means the Canadian government was given the power to amend its own constitution under specified rules. The law that allowed this change to happen became known as the Constitution Act, 1982.

Two very important additions to our constitution were made at this time:

- An amending formula, which sets out ways in which our constitution may be changed. The federal government and seven of the ten provinces must agree on the proposed amendment or change. Further, the seven provinces must make up at least one-half of the total population of Canada.

- The Charter of Rights and Freedoms, which outlines the basic rights and some of the responsibilities of all Canadians.

The Charter of Rights and Freedoms

As a Canadian citizen, you have certain fundamental freedoms and rights. They are guaranteed by a written document known as the Canadian Charter of Rights and Freedoms, which is part of the Canadian constitution. The Charter spells out a variety of rights in a series of points called articles.

Your basic freedoms and rights are preserved in the Canadian Charter of Rights and Freedoms, 1982.

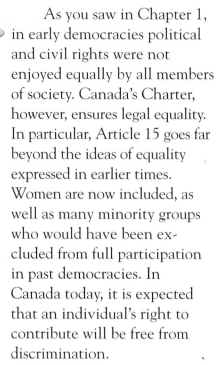

Excerpts from the Canadian Charter of Rights and Freedoms, 1982

Article 2:

Everyone has the following fundamental freedoms:

a) freedom of conscience and religion
b) freedom of thought, belief, opinion, and expression, including freedom of the press and other media of communication
c) freedom of peaceful assembly
d) freedom of association

Article 3:

Every citizen of Canada has the right to vote in an election of members of the House of Commons or of a legislative assembly and to be qualified for membership therein.

Article 7:

Everyone has the right to life, liberty, and security of the person.

Article 15:

Equality Rights: Every individual is equal before and under the law and has the right to equal protection and equal benefit of the law without discrimination and, in particular, without discrimination based on race, national or ethnic origin, colour, religion, sex, age, or mental or physical disability.

As you saw in Chapter 1, in early democracies political and civil rights were not enjoyed equally by all members of society. Canada's Charter, however, ensures legal equality. In particular, Article 15 goes far beyond the ideas of equality expressed in earlier times. Women are now included, as well as many minority groups who would have been excluded from full participation in past democracies. In Canada today, it is expected that an individual's right to contribute will be free from discrimination.

What role do you think the Charter plays in promoting social and economic equality?

ACTIVITIES THE INQUIRING CITIZEN

BE Informed

1. a) Identify and briefly describe the forces that affect how Canada is governed.
   b) Rank the top three factors. Explain how these factors might help to shape the others.

2. What is a constitution? What are the primary purposes of Canada's constitution? What changes were made in 1982?

3. Explain the purpose of the Charter of Rights and Freedoms, and Articles 2 and 15 specifically.

BE Purposeful

4. a) Interview three people. Ask "What is the most important thing that government does for you?" Record their responses.
   b) Report the responses to your class and then discuss the question, "Why does Canada need government?"

BE Active

5. Research one important historical episode in Canada's constitutional history. Your teacher will give you a list of possible choices. For your selection, describe two or three ideas that were introduced that influenced how Canada would be governed. Share your findings with your classmates.

Why Did Canada Adopt a Federal System of Government?

At the time of Confederation in 1867, the four colonies of British North America — Ontario (then called Canada West), Quebec (then called Canada East), Nova Scotia, and New Brunswick — were united to form the nation of Canada. The Fathers of Confederation knew that they couldn't create a single level of government that would work well for all of Canada. Given the different cultures, customs, and settlement histories that existed in each region, each province needed a way to address its unique concerns. In particular, the French-speaking community in Quebec wanted a way to protect their culture.

To provide for the different needs of the provinces, as well as the common needs of the entire nation, the Fathers of Confederation gave Canada a **federal system of government**. This meant that two levels of government were created. Decision-making power was divided between the national (federal) government based in Ottawa, and the regional (provincial) governments based in the capital city of every province.

federal system of government: A system of government in which powers and responsibilities are divided into national and regional levels to address national and regional needs.

Division of Power and Responsibilities

Our earliest constitutional planners wanted both to give the provinces a certain amount of control over regional issues and to create a strong national government. However, that did not mean that each level of government was given equal power. At the time of Confederation most power was given to the federal government.

Under section 91 of the Constitution Act, 1867 (BNA Act), the federal government was made responsible for matters that concerned the nation as a whole. Matters that require a consistent national policy — such as defence, dealings with other countries, currency, and a postal system — were put under the **jurisdiction** of the federal government.

jurisdiction: The authority to make and carry out laws.

In section 92 of the BNA Act, the provincial governments were given jurisdiction over areas that were best handled by those closer to the issues of the region. Such areas include education, environmental issues, medical care, social welfare, and labour legislation. The powers given to the four provincial governments were extended to other provinces at the time they joined Canada.

municipal government:
Governing body of a city or town.

In a further division of power, the provinces themselves have used their power to create **municipal governments**. This local level of government has the greatest amount of contact with individual citizens. It provides essential local services, such as garbage collection, sewage treatment, fire protection, water supply, and the establishment of schools.

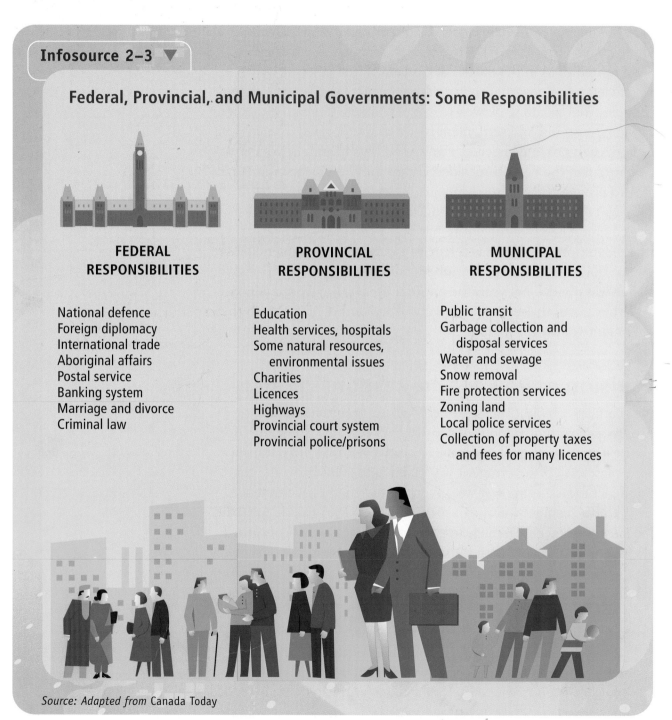

Infosource 2–3 ▼

Federal, Provincial, and Municipal Governments: Some Responsibilities

FEDERAL RESPONSIBILITIES

National defence
Foreign diplomacy
International trade
Aboriginal affairs
Postal service
Banking system
Marriage and divorce
Criminal law

PROVINCIAL RESPONSIBILITIES

Education
Health services, hospitals
Some natural resources, environmental issues
Charities
Licences
Highways
Provincial court system
Provincial police/prisons

MUNICIPAL RESPONSIBILITIES

Public transit
Garbage collection and disposal services
Water and sewage
Snow removal
Fire protection services
Zoning land
Local police services
Collection of property taxes and fees for many licences

Source: Adapted from Canada Today

Shared Powers and Residual Powers

Our constitution has areas of shared powers: the federal and provincial governments can both create laws regarding agriculture and immigration and some aspects of natural resources.
Overall, our constitution gives the federal level more power. Not only does it have broader listed powers, but areas that were not specifically listed were given to the federal government as **residual powers**.

These residual powers apply to new areas of jurisdiction that did not exist in 1867, such as telecommunications, cable television stations, computers, modems, and faxes. The writers of our constitution could not have predicted such advances in technology, yet they had the foresight to give control of "unknown possibilities" to the federal government.

residual powers: In Canada's constitution, any "leftover" powers that are not specifically listed, but remain with the federal government.

Why does this satellite disk fall under the category of residual powers?

ACTIVITIES — THE INQUIRING CITIZEN

BE Informed

1. In your own words, define "federal system of government." Why was government in Canada organized in this way?

2. **a)** Name three levels of government in Canada and describe what each level does.
   b) What is meant by "residual powers"? Which level of government is responsible for these powers?

3. Look back at the photographs on page 38. Which level of government is responsible for each of the services shown?

BE Purposeful

4. Make a chart of 10 activities in which you have been involved during the last week (e.g., going to school, playing a sport, listening to music). Beside each activity, identify:
   a) how government might be involved
   b) which level of government might be involved
   c) whom you might call if you needed more information about anything connected to this activity. You might find the blue pages of the telephone directory useful.

5. In your local newspaper, locate three stories connected to government. Choose one story for each of the three levels of government. For each, describe briefly:
   a) What is the issue?
   b) Who is involved? What different points of view exist?
   c) What level of government is responsible?
   d) What difficulties would the government face in making a decision on this issue?

CITIZEN'S TOOLKIT

Working Collaboratively

Before public decisions are made, the people involved often must come together to consider different points of view. There are many ways of working in a group, but here are some strategies that are effective in all cases.

- Be responsible for your own behaviour. For example, use your own ideas, try your best to do the tasks you have agreed to do, and admit it when you are unsure of what you have to do.

- Be respectful of others in the group. For example, listen to others, encourage others to participate by asking for their ideas, and express disagreement without putting other people down.

- Remember that everyone has abilities or skills that can contribute to completing the task.

Putting It Into Practice

1. Work in groups to answer one or two of the activities on page 45. Use the tips above to complete the steps below.

   a) Choose a "Reader" to read the first question aloud. Take turns sharing ideas about the answer. Do not write anything yet.
   b) The student to the left of the Reader should be the "Checker," who checks that everyone understands and agrees on an answer. When you have all agreed, each of you should write the answer in your own words.
   c) Move on to the second question, but rotate roles of Reader and Checker.
   d) At the end of the process, identify what worked well and how your group might improve next time.

2. Many activists work in groups. Why do you suppose that is the case? In which situations in your day-to-day life do you participate in collaborative groups? Which of the tips do you consider most helpful? Why?

Source: Adapted from Cooperative Learning and Social Studies

What Are the Traditions of Our Parliamentary System?

The written part of our constitution has been called the "skeleton" of our constitution. To put flesh on those bones, we must also consider less formal customs and practices in government decision making — our unwritten constitution. Historically, Canada has had strong ties to Great Britain and continues to use a similar system of government. Canada's highest decision-making body is its Parliament based on the British model. Canada's Parliament consists of the Queen, who is represented in Canada by the governor general; the Senate; and the House of Commons.

Constitutional Monarchy

Canada is a **constitutional monarchy**. Though we have our own constitution, we still recognize the British monarch (currently Queen Elizabeth II) as our own monarch and formal head of state. All federal acts (laws) passed by Parliament begin with the words: "Her Majesty, by and with the advice and consent of the Senate and the House of Commons, enacts as follows...." The key word here is "consent." Queen Elizabeth has very little real power in Canada today, but she is still part of our tradition.

constitutional monarchy: A government in which the monarch has only the powers laid out in the nation's constitution and laws.

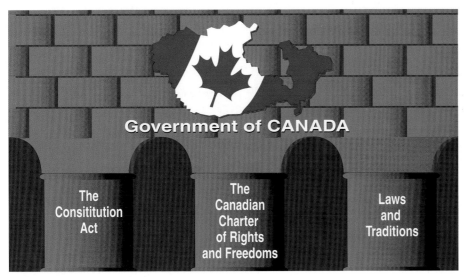

Source: *Adapted from* Canada Today

Above: The foundations of Canada's government. Tradition plays an important role in the way we are governed. **Right:** Queen Elizabeth II. Because Canada's monarch lives in Britain, he or she is represented here by the governor general.

The Governor General

The most important task of the governor general is to ensure that Canada has a government and a prime minister. Appointed by the monarch on the advice of the Canadian government, the governor general also performs formal functions. These include:

- opening Parliament and reading the Speech from the Throne, which outlines the ruling government's plans for that session of Parliament

- greeting foreign leaders and dignitaries

- formally acknowledging outstanding contributions of Canadians with awards and medals, such as the Order of Canada, the Cross of Valour, and the governor general's awards for literature

Representative Democracy

In a democracy, "the people," or at least the majority of "the people," have control over how decisions are made. This right to express yourself takes different forms. In *direct* forms of decision making, you participate directly in deciding the outcome of an issue or decision. In *representative* forms of decision making, your views or wishes are voiced by your representatives.

As you read in Chapter 1, in ancient Greece every eligible person participated directly in making every major political decision that affected the society. Such a system is known as **direct democracy**. The responsibility for being involved in decision making, as well as for abiding by the decisions, was held by each citizen.

In the complex societies we have today, however, it is no longer practical or possible for every citizen to make the many political decisions required each day. Instead, in Canada, citizens elect a representative to make decisions on their behalf. It is expected that representatives will listen to citizens and will be responsive to their interests. Elected representatives at all three levels of government — federal, provincial, and municipal — use the power given to them "by the people." Citizens, in turn, must participate actively to express their views to their representatives and to each other. In this way, power rests indirectly with the individual citizens of Canada. This system is known as indirect or **representative democracy**. In such a system, governments are encouraged to make good decisions so that citizens will re-elect them.

direct democracy: A democratic system in which every citizen participates directly in decision making.

representative democracy: A democratic system in which citizens vote for representatives who are empowered to make decisions on their behalf.

Adrienne Clarkson

Governor General

In 1999, Adrienne Clarkson was sworn in as Canada's 26th governor general and the second woman to hold this post. She is also the first person from a racial minority to hold this position.

Clarkson was born on February 10, 1939, in Hong Kong. When Hong Kong fell to the Japanese during World War II, she and her family fled to Canada as refugees. She was only three years old when she arrived in Ottawa in 1942. Growing up in an immigrant family, Clarkson developed a passionate interest in everything Canadian. She went on to study at the University of Toronto and at the Sorbonne in Paris, where she became fluent in French.

Clarkson began her career as a television journalist in 1965. In the early 1980s, she became one of the first women journalists to gain prominence on prime-time television in Canada. In 1982, Clarkson interrupted her career with the CBC to accept an appointment as Ontario's first agent-general in Paris. As agent-general, she promoted Canadian cultural and business interests in Europe, proving to be a skilled diplomat. She later returned to the CBC, where she wrote, hosted, and produced a series of television specials dedicated to

Canadian arts and culture. She received many awards for her work, as well as expanding her interests to include writing and producing films and documentaries.

As the Queen's representative, Clarkson celebrates the achievements of Canadians and encourages national unity and identity. Her appointment is a symbol of how diverse Canada has become. Having arrived in the city as a refugee, she returned to Ottawa to hold the country's highest public office.

Referendums

referendum: The process of referring a political question to the people for a direct vote.

One way that citizens in a complex modern society can exercise direct democracy in government is by **referendum**. In a referendum, citizens have the opportunity to express their opinions on a government proposal directly, by voting for or against it.

By the end of the twentieth century, the federal government had held only three referendums — always on matters of great national importance. For example, in 1992, a referendum was held on whether to accept the Charlottetown Accord, which would have made crucial changes to our constitution. Seventy-five per cent of eligible voters participated. The vote was 54.2 per cent against and 44.8 per cent for. The Charlottetown Accord was not accepted because of the Canadian people's decision.

Provinces and local governments also use referendums from time to time. For instance, one very important referendum in Newfoundland in 1948 brought about its decision to join Confederation as the tenth province. Quebec has had two referendums, in 1980 and 1995, to determine the province's political future within Canada.

The 1980 Quebec referendum provoked strong differences in opinion.

ACTIVITIES   THE INQUIRING CITIZEN

BE Informed

1. Describe two traditions of our parliamentary system.
2. **a)** How is direct democracy different from representative democracy?
   b) List three examples of groups you belong to (e.g., a school club). For each, explain whether it is an example of direct democracy, representative democracy, or autocratic decision making. Which form of decision making do you prefer? Why?
3. What is a referendum? On what kinds of issues are referendums called?

BE Purposeful

4. **a)** Compare the roles of the monarch and the governor general.
   b) What three qualities do you think are important in a governor general?
   c) How might Adrienne Clarkson's background help her to be an effective governor general?

5. Some people believe the Queen is too distant to be relevant to Canadians. Others believe she has an important role to play. Debate: Canada should abolish the monarchy.

Why Is Canadian Citizenship Important?

Citizenship in Canada allows you to share in the privileges, rights, and freedoms — as well as the obligations — of membership in our democratic nation. Our rights and responsibilities can be summarized briefly as follows:

- Individuals are free within common limits to live as they see fit.
- Individuals have a responsibility to respect those same freedoms of others.

The meaning of Canadian citizenship is still evolving. The expectations of how we should behave as responsible citizens have become more complex. For example, as pollution has become a prime issue, many Canadians have come to expect their neighbours to behave in ways that are more environmentally responsible.

Who Is Considered a Canadian Citizen?

The first Canadian Citizenship Act, in 1947, outlined who could be a Canadian citizen. People born within the boundaries of Canada were granted Canadian citizenship. So, too, were children of a Canadian father who were born in a foreign nation. Those who wished to immigrate and become Canadian citizens were required to meet certain conditions. These conditions varied for different people.

In 1977, a new Canadian Citizenship Act was passed, which was fairer. The basis of this Act is similar to the Charter of Rights and Freedoms: all people are entitled to equal and fair treatment in their dealings with the government of Canada. Today, the Canada Act (1982) and the Canadian Charter of Rights and Freedoms (1982) outline many of the expectations of citizenship in Canada.

A person is considered a Canadian citizen if he or she is born in Canada or if one parent is Canadian. Someone who is not a Canadian citizen by birth may become a citizen through the legal process known as "naturalization." To become a Canadian citizen, you must:

- be 18 years or older
- be a permanent resident who was lawfully admitted to Canada

> **Did You Know?**
>
> Canada has been a nation since 1867, but citizenship in Canada is just over 50 years old. Until the Canadian Citizenship Act came into being in 1947, Canadians were considered British subjects, not Canadian citizens.

- have lived here for three out of the previous four years

- speak either English or French

- know the information about Canada outlined in the Citizenship and Immigration Canada handbook, *A Look at Canada*

If the applicant meets all these conditions, he or she swears the oath of allegiance to the Queen and becomes a citizen.

These immigrants, at the turn of the twentieth century, are studying to become Canadian citizens. How does this group differ from the group of new citizens shown below?

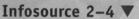

Infosource 2–4 ▼

Oath of Canadian Citizenship

I swear (or affirm) that I will be faithful
and bear true allegiance to Her Majesty,
Queen Elizabeth the Second,
Queen of Canada,
Her Heirs and Successors,
and that I will faithfully observe
the laws of Canada
and fulfill my duties as a Canadian citizen.

Who Can Participate in Electing a Representative?

Today, nearly every adult Canadian citizen has the right to participate in an election to vote for his or her representative. The right to vote, called the **franchise**, gives citizens one of their important roles in the democratic decision-making process. When Canadians vote, they do so by secret ballot, which means that a voter's choice can remain strictly private if she or he wishes. This long-standing practice exists to discourage both the bribery and intimidation of voters.

However, not every adult Canadian has always had the franchise. For many groups of people, it was a hard-won democratic right. For example, even 50 years after Confederation, women were completely disenfranchised (deprived of the right to vote). It took the involvement

franchise: The right to vote in a public election for members of Parliament, provincial legislatures, and municipal councils.

This illustration shows an election before the advent of the secret ballot. Canadian voters used to have to stand and declare their vote in public.

suffrage movement: The campaign for women's right to vote.

of women in the **suffrage movement** to educate and influence the public about women's status as equal members of society. Finally, by 1918, the suffragists gained enough support to win the right to vote in federal elections. Through the first half of the twentieth century, most Asian Canadians and Aboriginal Canadians were still denied the vote. It took many more years for the franchise to be extended to racial minority groups.

After gaining the franchise in federal elections, women still had to win the right to vote in provincial elections. As late as 1940, Quebec became the last province to grant women the franchise. Meanwhile there were other battles to be fought. In order for women to become representatives in government, they first had to be legally defined as "persons" — citizens with the right to hold office.

Did You Know?

Secret ballots were first used in New Brunswick in 1855, twelve years before Confederation.

This Chinese couple is voting in the 1963 general election, when for the first time, the federal franchise was free of racial and religious discrimination.

At one time, it was difficult to conduct elections in the North and in other sparsely populated areas of Canada. Today, technologies such as fax machines, as well as the special ballot for mail-in registration and voting, have made the process easier.

1867

Only men who own property are allowed to vote.

1880s – 1890s

Thousands of people hold meetings, organize rallies, sign petitions, and donate money to gain the franchise for Canadian women.

1885

The Electoral Franchise Act defines a "person" as a male. All people of Asian descent are excluded.

1916

Women in Manitoba become the first in Canada to win the right to vote in provincial elections (see Infosource 2–6).

1917

The Wartime Election Act takes away the right to vote from Canadian citizens who were born in an enemy country and obtained citizenship after March 1902. Those whose first language or parents' language is the language of an enemy country also lose the right to vote.

Wives, sisters, and mothers of servicemen win the vote in federal elections. The right to vote is extended to Aboriginal Canadians in the armed forces.

1918

All adult women win the right to vote in federal elections, except those of Asian, Inuit, or Status Indian descent.

1934

All Inuit lose the right to vote.

1948

The vote is extended to Japanese Canadians, the last Asian Canadians to receive the franchise.

1950

Inuit become eligible to vote.

1960

The Indian Act is amended to extend the vote to Aboriginal Canadians living on reserves.

1970

The voting age is reduced from 21 to 18.

1987

Judges become eligible to vote.

1988

People with mental disabilities are granted the right to vote.

1992

Voting rights are extended to prison inmates.

1999

Prison inmates lose their right to vote.

Emily Murphy and the Famous Five
The 1929 Persons Case

Emily Murphy

At the turn of the twentieth century, suffragists fought to get a woman appointed to the Senate, part of the Canadian legislature. The Constitution Act, 1867 (BNA Act), stated that "the Governor General shall…summon qualified persons to the Senate." Their opponents argued that within the statutes of British common law, women were not "persons" and therefore could not hold public office.

In 1927, five women presented a petition to the Supreme Court of Canada, challenging the exclusion of women in the legal term "person." These five women were all from Alberta. Emily Murphy, Nellie McClung, Louise McKinney, Henrietta Muir Edwards, and Irene Parlby were well-known suffragists committed to the cause of women's rights. Together they became known as the Famous Five.

When the petition was brought before the Supreme Court of Canada in March 1928, it became known as the Persons Case. In April, the court ruled that women were not regarded as persons under the BNA Act and could therefore not hold a seat in the Senate. Discouraged but not defeated, the Famous Five appealed the decision to the Judicial Committee of the British Privy Council in London, England, which was at that time Canada's final court of appeal.

In 1929, the Privy Council overturned the ruling of Canada's Supreme Court. It ruled that women were indeed persons and therefore were qualified to become members of the Canadian Senate. Thanks to the Famous Five, women could no longer be legally excluded from any public office in Canada.

Infosource 2–6 ▼

Women's Eligibility to Vote and Hold Office in Provincial Elections

Province	Vote Granted[1]	Eligible to Hold Office	First Woman Elected
Manitoba	Jan. 28, 1916	same	June 29, 1920
Saskatchewan	Mar. 14, 1916	same	June 29, 1919
Alberta	Apr. 19, 1916	same	June 7, 1917
BC	Apr. 5, 1917	same	Jan. 24, 1918
Ontario	Apr. 23, 1917	Apr. 4, 1919	Aug. 4, 1943
Nova Scotia	Apr. 26, 1918	same	June 7, 1960
New Brunswick	Apr. 17, 1919	Mar. 9, 1934	Oct. 10, 1967
PEI	May 3, 1922	same	May 11, 1970
Newfoundland[2]	Apr. 13, 1925	same	May 17, 1930
Quebec	Apr. 25, 1940	same	Dec. 15, 1961

[1]Note that Aboriginal and Asian women, like Aboriginal and Asian men, did not have the same rights as other women.

[2]While men could vote at 21, women had to wait until they were 25. This legislation remained until Newfoundland's entry into Confederation in 1948.

Source: Adapted from The Gilded Ghetto

ACTIVITIES   THE INQUIRING CITIZEN

BE Informed

1. What is meant by the franchise?

2. Name four groups of citizens who were not allowed to vote in Canada in the first half of the twentieth century.

BE Purposeful

3. Review Infosources 2–5 and 2–6. Has democracy always been "by the people" in Canada? Provide three pieces of evidence to support your point of view.

4. **a)** In your view, is it important in a democracy that every citizen have the right to vote? Explain.

b) Are there certain groups in Canada that are denied the right to vote, even today? Explain.

BE Active

5. Assume you live in the year 1917. Prepare a political poster in which you try to persuade the public about why women or other groups denied the vote should be given the franchise. On the reverse side of the poster, prepare a paragraph that explains its design and content.

Should Canadians Under 18 Be Eligible to Vote?

Many young people are interested in changing our society, both to suit their own needs and to address such issues as injustice, inequality, and environmental damage. As the future leaders of Canada, high-school-aged citizens could have a greater influence on Canadian politics if they were given the right to vote. Although the Charter of Rights and Freedoms (Article 3) guarantees all citizens the right to vote in elections, lawmakers have used the Charter's clause of "reasonable limits" (Article 1) to limit young people under the age of 18 from

Infosource 2–7 ▼

WHAT THE CHARTER SAYS ABOUT THE RIGHT TO VOTE

Article 3:
Every citizen of Canada has the right to vote in an election of members of the House of Commons or of a legislative assembly....

Article 1:
The Canadian Charter of Rights and Freedoms guarantees the rights and freedoms set out in it subject only to such *reasonable limits* prescribed by law as can be demonstrably justified in a free and democratic society.

Infosource 2–8 ▼

ELECTORAL MATURITY

What are the characteristics of "electoral maturity"? It consists of being capable of making an informed judgment on the past performance of a government and candidate, on their programs, and on their ability to deliver on their campaign promises.... It is necessary to keep informed, to take part in meetings and to dialogue with fellow citizens. A citizen who can do this has the desired electoral maturity.

Can it be demonstrated that 17- or 16-year-olds would not have this electoral maturity? When they are legally freed from parental authority or in business, they are treated on equal footing with adults. They may hold a job, pay taxes, and freely carry out many legal acts.... With the required consent they can marry, have family responsibilities, drive a vehicle, and join the armed forces....

Patrice Garant, Carleton University researcher

Source: Youth in Canadian Politics: Participation and Involvement

having this right. In addition, the Canada Election Act limits the right to vote to "adults." Some people, however, believe that 16- and 17-year-olds should be eligible to vote.

If 16-year-olds are responsible enough to drive, does that mean they are mature enough to vote?

YOUNG DRIVERS OF CANADA

Infosource 2–9 ▼

FOUR OBJECTIONS TO LOWERING THE VOTING AGE

1. Young people are not knowledgeable about political affairs — they would not know a good policy from a bad one.
2. Children should not be considered responsible electors (voters) because they may cast their vote frivolously.
3. Children are more likely to vote on the basis of the personality of the candidate than the policies that the candidate stands for.
4. Parents might seek to influence their children and force them to vote according to their preferences.

Source: Adapted from The Rights of Children

ANALYZING THE ISSUE

BE **Purposeful**

1. **a)** What is the issue discussed here?
    b) Make a chart listing arguments for and against lowering the voting age. Rank the arguments from most to least persuasive.
    c) Compare your results with a partner's. What do you think accounts for the similarities or differences in your opinions?

2. **a)** Think of some arguments of your own, either for or against lowering the voting age.
    b) Predict how adults or others outside your school might feel on the issue. Give reasons for your view.
    c) Ask four or five people outside your class for their opinion. Were your predictions correct?

BE **Active**

3. Is restricting the right to vote to people over 18 a "reasonable limit" (see Infosource 2–7)?
    a) Discuss in a small group.
    b) Present your group's point of view to the class. Possible formats include a radio commercial, information video, public service announcement, or skit.

Determining Facts and Opinions

Most information that you observe or hear can be classified either as a fact or an opinion.

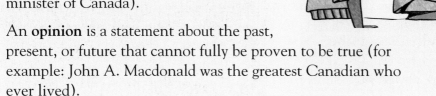

- A **fact** is an exact statement about something that has really happened and can be investigated and verified to be true (for example: John A. Macdonald was the first prime minister of Canada).

- An **opinion** is a statement about the past, present, or future that cannot fully be proven to be true (for example: John A. Macdonald was the greatest Canadian who ever lived).

Putting It Into Practice

1. Identify the characteristics of a fact and an opinion.

2. Copy the following statements into your notebook. For each, assess whether it is a fact or an opinion, and briefly explain why.

   a) Article 3 of the Canadian Charter of Rights and Freedoms states that all citizens are guaranteed the right to vote in elections.
   b) High-school-aged citizens could dramatically reshape Canadian politics if they were given the right to vote.
   c) Children are more likely to vote on the basis of the personality of the candidate than the policies that the candidate stands for.
   d) People who are 16 or 17 years old may hold a job, pay taxes, and carry out legal acts.
   e) Our Charter rights are subject to reasonable limits.

3. With a partner, compare your responses. As a class, discuss what difficulties you encountered in distinguishing between a fact and an opinion.

4. Why is it important to be able to know the difference between facts and opinions in everyday life? How might knowing the difference help a citizen exercise his or her rights in a democracy?

How Do Democratic Governments Promote "the Common Good"?

Democratic governments are responsible for taking action to promote the common good. But how do they know what is in the best interest of a whole community? Usually, "the common good" means the greatest good for the greatest number of people.

To make wise decisions that satisfy the majority of citizens, government representatives need to listen carefully to what the people they represent have to say. There is no other accurate source of information about what citizens want and need. Similarly, citizens in a democracy must be able to voice their ideas and opinions to governments. Good communication between government and citizens is an important part of democracy.

In a democracy, citizens can voice their opinions through voting in elections. However, voting is only one of several ways that citizens participate and make their views known to other citizens and to governments. A great variety of political activity happens between elections. In fact, we could not have a democratic civil society if citizens became active only at election time. Democratic societies depend on people exercising their democratic rights on an ongoing basis.

Citizens have various democratic rights that allow them to make their voices heard. These rights include freedom of expression and freedom of association. These rights and freedoms are considered so important they are included in our Charter of Rights and Freedoms.

Often, freedom of expression and association are expressed in **social movements**, groups of concerned citizens who campaign for what they believe is right. These movements play an important role in communicating wants and needs to people in power. With their demands for social justice, they have brought about many changes in Canadian society.

These chemical workers, circa 1947, are on strike. What rights were these women exercising? What do you think they achieved?

social movement: Organized campaign by large groups of concerned citizens to lobby or otherwise influence the government.

CHANGING VIEWS OF SOCIAL JUSTICE AND RIGHTS IN CANADA

Let's go back 100 years to examine the demands made by the labour movement in Canada. The following were their goals, considered extremely radical and unachievable at the time:

- free elementary education
- a [maximum] 60 hours (work) week for women and children over 12

- the elimination of the master and servant law, which imposed prison terms on people who quit their jobs without their employer's permission
- the extension of the vote beyond property owners

Source: The Power of Social Movements

Citizen Participation

Because governments cannot meet citizens' needs without their input, it is important for individuals, groups of citizens, and social movements to participate actively. But how often do they do so? Which Canadian citizens are most likely to become involved in their communities and what are they most likely to do?

How Extensively Do Canadian Citizens Participate?

- About 10 per cent of Canadians "appear completely disengaged politically" — they don't vote or take any interest in public affairs.
- Another 25 to 30 per cent limit themselves to voting and talking about politics.
- The remainder — who at 50 to 65 per cent are in the majority — not only vote but also get involved in political life, at least sometimes, in some other way.

- In the last 50 years, an average of 75 per cent of eligible voters have cast their votes in Canadian federal elections.
- About 60 per cent of Canadians are members of one or more voluntary organizations or groups such as labour unions, professional associations, and church or fraternal groups, which are involved in political affairs.

Source: Canadian Politics in the 1990s

How are these citizens participating?

Even today, after many democratic rights have been won, the amount and type of citizen participation varies greatly. A variety of factors — including age, education, gender, income, and occupation — appear to influence who participates.

It is also true that, even when citizens do participate, the results are varied. Sometimes governments give citizens more opportunity to make their voices heard, and sometimes they seem to pay little attention to the wishes of some people. Citizens sometimes have a great impact on the way decisions are made, but sometimes they make very little difference at all.

How can we know if we are making a difference by participating? Sometimes government decisions and policies can be changed by citizens who make their views known. At other times, we can measure the results of our actions in different ways. We can say that we have made a difference:

- if we have not been ignored
- if we have had some influence, even if it has not been as great as we had hoped
- if we have managed to change a decision, even if we do not get exactly what we wanted
- if we have been part of a process in which everyone feels his or her voice was heard and in which everyone had an equal opportunity to make a difference

Infosource 2–12 ▼

DIFFERENT DEGREES OF PARTICIPATION

Making no difference  **Making a significant difference**

| Citizens are ignored by government. | Citizens have some influence on government decisions. | Citizens are treated as equals in the decision-making process. |

ACTIVITIES   THE INQUIRING CITIZEN

BE Informed

1. a) What is meant by "the common good"?

b) Governments eventually agreed to the demands of the labour movement outlined in Infosource 2–10. How did each of these goals support the common good?

2. a) According to Infosource 2–11, to what extent do Canadian citizens participate?

b) List some of the ways in which citizens in Canada can make their voices heard.

c) Think of a decision that was recently made in your family, school, or community. To what extent did you participate in the decision making? Where would you locate your participation on the scale shown in Infosource 2–12?

BE Purposeful

3. a) Describe what you think are three goals for the common good in our society today.

b) Imagine what the world will be like 50 years from now. Predict how ideas about the common good might change.

Should Cyclists Be Required to Wear Helmets by Law?

Even when citizens are actively involved in decision making about a public issue, it can be difficult for governments to determine the common good — to decide what is in the best interests of the greatest number of people. The views of citizens on some issues may be very different or even contradictory. Consider the issue of bicycle helmets.

The provincial governments of Ontario and British Columbia passed laws requiring cyclists to wear helmets on public streets. Those who disobey the laws are fined. Both laws were passed for the sake of "public safety" — or the common good. Yet both laws are controversial and have provoked public reaction.

What is this cartoon trying to say? Is it effective? Why or why not?

The Bicycle Helmet Debate

Helmet hair is not a pretty sight, but cracked skulls are even uglier. That's why the province's decision to make bike helmets mandatory...is the right one.... First, when there is an identifiable risk to public safety, the government has a responsibility to take steps to minimize that risk even if those measures interfere with individual rights.... Second, taxpayers shouldn't foot the bill when bike riders who like to feel the wind rushing through their hair end the trip in hospital with a fractured skull.

Editorial, Vancouver Sun

I, too, have been persuaded by the evidence that bicycle helmets are a good idea.... [But does that mean that] helmet-less cycling [is] enough of a serious threat to our community to rank the use of government force? ... Our governments already bully us too much. Do-gooders should learn to treat us as people capable of making good choices instead of mindless dolts ready to be controlled.

Paul Geddes, Greater Vancouver Libertarian Association, Vancouver Sun

[G]overnment studies [show] that bicycle helmets can reduce fatalities in accidents by 75 per cent and head injuries by 85 per cent. The Ontario Medical Association has long supported the protective gear.

Editorial, Toronto Star

I don't like the proposed new mandatory helmet law. I am 11 years old and don't want to have to wear a stupid helmet every time I go out on my bike.... I belong to a family of five so that's $500 for five helmets.

Brian Clow, Toronto Star

This injured cyclist was not wearing his helmet when he was hit by a car and thrown about 10 metres.

ANALYZING THE ISSUE

BE Informed

1. **a)** What political event is shown in the cartoon on page 65?
   b) What message does the cartoon present about public safety and the common good?
   c) Do you think the cartoon is effective in getting its message across? Explain.

BE Purposeful

2. **a)** List the arguments for and against the mandatory bicycle helmet law.
   b) Which of these views do you think best represents the common good? Why?

3. What do you think governments should do when there is no widespread agreement about which decision best serves the common good?

The Freedom to Disagree

As you saw in the case study on the helmet laws, when people disagree strongly with decisions made by political authorities, they sometimes challenge them. In democratic systems, citizens are able to express discontent with the outcome of the decision-making process. They have the right to appeal and the right to associate with others to oppose decisions made by the government. These rights are guaranteed by the Charter of Rights and Freedoms, because they are believed to promote the common good.

Infosource 2–14 ▼

Student expelled for leading protest

A student has been kicked out of high school for organizing a protest against university tuition hikes. Tom Keefer, 17, says he has been told not to return to his school because the protest was considered a disturbance. He was also cited for "consistent opposition to authority" and conduct that is "injurious to the morals" of the school.

Keefer led students on a noisy, two-hour demonstration through several Guelph high schools. It was similar to a protest held in Ottawa at the same time that was aimed at raising awareness of a cross-Canada student demonstration. The Canadian Federation of Students plans to fight to get Keefer back into school. Political action by students, whether or not school administration agree with their opinion, should be encouraged, said a CFS spokesperson.

Source: Adapted from Toronto Star

Students sometimes take to the streets in order to get the government's attention, and to ensure their voices are heard.

Challenging a Deportation Order

When Kathy-Ann Roopchan took to the stage of George Harvey Collegiate...it was to receive the recognition, praise, and support of

her peers. It may also have been to say goodbye.

Roopchan, 18, her mother and two younger sisters are facing deportation back to their homeland of Trinidad — despite the family's strong desire to stay. The Roopchan family has been in Canada [for seven years], but when the family's refugee claim was denied last February, a formal deportation order was issued.

"All my friends are here, my family is here," Roopchan said, wiping tears from her eyes after fellow students and staff delivered moving tributes to her. "Canada is my home now." Roopchan, now in her final year in high school, was last year's student council president. She has won the school's Terry Fox Award two years in a row for raising the most money for cancer research. And a letter from Northwestern Hospital says she has spent 130 hours of volunteer time there.

A raucous assembly of students — some waving signs saying "Kathy should stay" — gathered in the auditorium to show their support for Roopchan. Many also pledged to accompany her today when she tries to meet with the Immigration Minister at his office.

Source: Adapted from Toronto Star

ACTIVITIES — THE INQUIRING CITIZEN

BE Informed

1. What are the problems faced by each of the following, and who has offered support?
   a) Tom Keefer
   b) Kathy-Ann Roopchan

BE Purposeful

2. Does Tom Keefer's right to express his disagreement with government decisions include the right to organize a protest demonstration in local high schools? Why or why not?

3. In what ways does Infosource 2–15 suggest that allowing Kathy-Ann Roopchan to stay would serve the common good?

4. Do you believe that the right to disagree promotes the common good? Explain.

BE Informed

1. Use each of the following terms in a sentence, taking care to show how the term is connected to democratic citizenship in Canada.
   a) constitution
   b) federal system
   c) franchise
   d) direct democracy
   e) residual powers
   f) referendum
   g) social movement

2. In your own words, describe who is or who may become a Canadian citizen.

BE Purposeful

3. Choose one person or group that has made a difference to the evolution of Canada's democratic system of government. Research this person or group and write a profile describing how he, she, or it made a difference. Explain the values expressed by this person's or group's actions. Possible subjects include:
   - Nellie McClung
   - Japanese Canadian Committee for Democracy
   - Louis Riel
   - J. S. Woodsworth
   - Canadian Civil Liberties Association
   - National Action Committee on the Status of Women
   - Ovide Mercredi
   - David Lam
   - Rosemary Brown

BE Active

4. In groups of four, prepare to argue one of the following issues:
   - Should there be a law making it mandatory for all citizens to vote in elections?
   - Should governments allow citizens to make their own decisions about whether to wear bicycle helmets?
   - Should people under the age of 18 be given the right to vote?

   a) Divide into pairs, each taking a different point of view. Prepare your arguments based on information in this chapter and any other research you have completed.

   b) Share your ideas with others in the class who are taking the same position. Add any new arguments to your own.

   c) In your group of four, present your arguments. Follow the guidelines for a good argument:
   - Criticize ideas, not people.
   - Listen, even when you disagree.
   - Try to understand all sides of the issue.
   - Be willing to change your mind if the evidence convinces you.
   - Go for the best decision, not victory.

   d) Reverse your position. Continue the discussion in your group of four.

   e) Now decide what you really think about the issue. Try to reach a decision you all agree on. Remember the tips for working collaboratively.

   f) Prepare a two-minute ad or write a letter to the editor giving your view.

   Source: Adapted from Creative Controversy

5. With a partner, choose an individual or group that is involved in political action in your community. Possibilities include:
   - a political party
   - a public interest group (e.g., a human rights group)
   - a public agency (e.g., the chamber of commerce in your town, a food bank)
   - an individual involved in a specific political action

   a) Read any relevant literature, visit Web sites, or speak to people to find out:
   - what the individual or group stands for
   - what types of issues and activities the person or group is involved in
   - how the person or group is part of the political system
   - how you might get involved
   - what skills you would need to get involved, or what skills you would learn by participating

   b) Prepare a display of posters, pictures, or other information to communicate your findings. Invite teachers, other students, parents, and community members to view and discuss your display.

3 Participating at the Local Level

The Informed Citizen

How do municipal governments serve people in their communities? What are the challenges?

How are decisions made and conflicts resolved at the municipal level?

How can you keep informed about issues in your community?

The Purposeful Citizen

Why is it important to know about local issues?

Do municipal governments respond fairly to all citizens?

The Active Citizen

How can citizens voice their points of view at the local level?

How does participating at the local level help put democracy into action?

Whether you live in the city, in a town, or in the country, you have needs that must be met, such as access to clean drinking water, transportation, and garbage collection. These are some of the essential services that your local, or municipal, government provides.

Municipal government is the form of government that is closest to the people. At this level, citizens have the greatest opportunity to voice opinions on government decisions and to make a difference to the outcome of an issue. Participating at a local level is your right and your responsibility — and an important aspect of living in a democracy.

In this chapter, you will explore democracy at the local level. You will consider how local government attempts to serve community needs. In addition, you will look at what it means for local decision makers to hear, involve, and represent the people they are elected to serve. You will also examine why it is important for ordinary citizens to participate in politics at the local level.

Key Terms

- **municipality**
- **metropolitan government**
- **amalgamation**
- **school board**
- **civil service**
- **bylaws**
- **local planning**
- **grassroots organizing**

WHAT DO **YOU** THINK?

Billboards and street ads are designed to attract our attention. Many are interesting and attractive. Some, however, can be controversial.

From the window of her apartment, Deanne Taylor could see an ad that offended her. Fifteen metres high, it featured the back view of an almost bare man, in an ad for jeans. When Taylor phoned City Hall to complain, she found that the advertising company had not obtained permission to put the poster up. Also, the poster was larger than local government regulations allowed. The municipal government ordered the company to take it down.

The company argued against this order. It released a statement describing Deanne Taylor as a "whiner." The statement also said that "there is only one reason cities exist. Commerce.

Every city exists for the sole purpose of making money. Every other element is simply a side effect."

■ Explain why the ad for jeans became an issue. What were Deanne Taylor's concerns? What was the company's response?

■ Do you think Deanne Taylor was serving the city, as well as herself, by her actions?

■ The company argued that cities exist to promote commerce. Do you think the company was serving the city, as well as itself?

■ If you were a government official who had to decide on this issue, how would you respond? Explain.

■ Why is it important for politicians to respond to citizens' complaints?

How Do Municipal Governments Serve Their Communities?

As you read in Chapter 2, municipal, or local, government was created by the provinces for practical purposes. Local governments were set up to deliver the basic services to people with common needs living in a community.

Origins of Local Government Services in Canada

In Canada, the tradition of local government began with Aboriginal people in the form of band councils led by a chief responsible to the people. The first non-Aboriginal local governments in Canada emerged in response to immigration and settlement. The centralized colonial governments found they could not take care of this growing population, scattered over vast areas of land. Larger groups of settlers, especially in urban areas, required more services. The practical solution was to establish local authorities to make decisions on matters that they understood first-hand.

Infosource 3–1 ▼

Local Laws

NEW FRANCE, April 21, 1664 — The sovereign council today passed the first hygiene law in New France. It aims to protect public health by banning "straw, manure, and everything else" from being thrown on the streets.

Source: Historical Atlas of Canada

Infosource 3–2 ▼

Early Basic Services

CHARLOTTETOWN, December 21, 1885 — Last fall the council hired Royal Electric of Montreal to update street lighting here. Tonight the town switches on the first electric lights on PEI. Most applaud the move. *The Examiner* writes, "There is no doubt that ere long electricity will become as familiar to us as gas or kerosene, and it behooves us to keep pace with the times and not remain forever in our sleepy hollow."

Source: Historical Atlas of Canada

The form of local government that evolved in Canada was shaped by the United Empire Loyalists, who fled from New York and the New England colonies in the 1780s and brought many of their traditions to Canada. In the United States, they had enjoyed the local tradition of the "town meeting." Each year, citizens of the town who lived within one kilometre of the meeting house elected representatives to deal with the town's affairs and to look after the basic needs of the townspeople.

October 11, 1910: Citizens of Berlin (now Kitchener), Ontario, cheer as hydro power is turned on for the first time.

Although immigration increased over time, cities in British North America remained relatively small. When Canada was formed in 1867, only about one out of ten citizens lived in a city over 10 000 people. Local governments were established to provide the essential basic services — such as fire fighting, police protection, road maintenance, and utilities. A city, town, county, district, township, or other community that had its own local government became known as a **municipality**.

municipality: A city, town, county, district, township, or other community area having local self-government.

ACTIVITIES   THE INQUIRING CITIZEN

BE **Informed**

1. Describe briefly how and why municipal governments started in Canada.

2. Examine Infosources 3–1 and 3–2.
   a) What local needs were being met in each case?
   b) How does your community today address the same needs?

BE **Purposeful**

3. Town meetings were a forum to elect town officials, but what other needs do you suppose town meetings might have satisfied?

Today's Essential Local Services

Today, over three-quarters of all Canadians live in urban settings. As towns and cities have grown, municipal governments have had to provide more services for larger populations. The basics — such as a clean water supply, utilities, and waste disposal — are no longer enough. Today, people expect additional services that they consider essential to our much more complex lives. In our modern, industrialized, computerized society, daily service expectations are far greater than they were in the past. Which of the services shown in Infosource 3–4 do you and your family use?

Funding for Local Services

The services provided by municipal governments are essential, expected, and expensive. They are a major part of all municipal budgets. Funding to pay for municipal services is raised mostly from property taxes — taxes on houses, apartments, and businesses in the municipality. Additional funds are received from user fees, such as licences and parking permits.

Sometimes provincial governments contribute funding for areas where they share the responsibility, such as public transportation and schools. Provincial governments also provide grants to municipalities, though the number and the amounts of these grants have recently been decreasing.

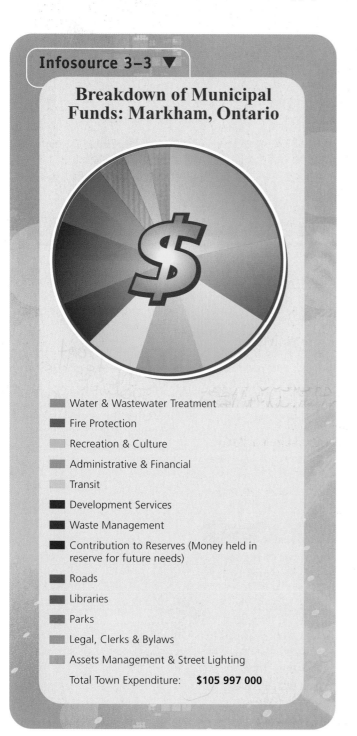

Infosource 3–3 ▼

Breakdown of Municipal Funds: Markham, Ontario

- Water & Wastewater Treatment
- Fire Protection
- Recreation & Culture
- Administrative & Financial
- Transit
- Development Services
- Waste Management
- Contribution to Reserves (Money held in reserve for future needs)
- Roads
- Libraries
- Parks
- Legal, Clerks & Bylaws
- Assets Management & Street Lighting

Total Town Expenditure: **$105 997 000**

Infosource 3–4 ▼

Some Modern Local Government Services

ambulance service
animal control
child care
community centres
facilities for the disabled
homeless shelters
libraries
medical clinics
parks and recreation
poison and paint disposal
public housing
public transit
recycling services
seniors facilities and services
traffic control

ACTIVITIES   THE INQUIRING CITIZEN

BE Informed

1. Examine Infosource 3–3. List the three areas where the most money is spent.

BE Purposeful

2. **a)** With a partner, visit your local government's Web site at the Intergovernmental On-Line Information Kiosk (www.intergov.gc.ca/) and record the services offered by your local government.

   b) With your partner, find newspaper stories, cartoons, and editorials that deal with local government services.

   c) As a class, create a bulletin board display of local government services. Contact your local government for more information to display.

BE Active

3. Obtain a copy of the budget for your municipality. Contact your municipal government offices or use the Internet. Compare the budget with that of Markham (Infosource 3–3). How are the budgets similar and different? What do you think accounts for the similarities and differences?

How Are Municipal Governments Organized?

Municipal governments in Canada take many forms. Whether your municipal area is called a township, village, town, or city generally depends on the number of people who live there. The boundary for your municipal area is set by the provincial government.

The responsibilities of municipal governments vary somewhat from province to province. For example, Prince Edward Island's small size makes it practical for the provincial government to handle many local needs that municipal governments handle in provinces with larger populations.

In rural areas, towns and sparsely populated communities sometimes collaborate to provide common services more efficiently. These combined communities may form districts, counties, or regions.

In urban centres with large populations, neighbouring municipalities also sometimes join together to provide services more efficiently. This form of government is known as **metropolitan government**. The metropolitan government handles shared services for the

metropolitan government: A form of municipal government that provides common services to citizens of several neighbouring municipalities.

This cartoon comments on amalgamation in Halifax, Nova Scotia. What comment does it make?

metropolitan area. Within the metropolitan area, local municipalities keep control of local matters. For example, a metropolitan government often provides public transportation or sewage systems. Local municipalities provide services such as snow plowing or maintenance of parks and recreation.

The first metropolitan government in Canada was set up in the early 1950s in the Toronto area. Later, similar governments were created in Halifax, Montreal, Winnipeg, and other Canadian cities. In more recent years, municipalities have combined to provide more shared services in a process known as **amalgamation**. In an amalgamated city, one metropolitan government handles all local services. Toronto, Winnipeg, and Halifax all became amalgamated cities in the late 1990s. In 1999, the Ontario provincial government passed legislation to create amalgamated cities in Ottawa and Hamilton, as well. While some people believe that amalgamated cities can provide services in a more economical and efficient manner, others believe that smaller municipalities are more effective.

amalgamation: The combination of cities, towns, or other areas under one government.

What can you tell about the varying sizes of municipal governments from these photographs?

Citizens for Local Democracy

Citizens for Local Democracy was founded in 1996, when the Ontario provincial government announced controversial plans to make Toronto an amalgamated city, or "megacity."

The municipality of metropolitan Toronto had been created in 1953 to provide common services in the area. At the same time, 13 local municipalities continued to deliver local services. Over time, the 13 local municipalities were amalgamated into five cities and one borough: Toronto, York, Scarborough, Etobicoke, North York, and East York. The metropolitan government continued to provide area-wide services.

The 1996 plan called for the further amalgamation of these seven municipalities into a single City of Toronto government. Supporters of the plan argued that amalgamation would lower the costs of providing services to the country's largest urban area. They also said that amalgamation was the next logical step in a process that began in 1953. Opponents argued that citizens would lose their connection with local government. The 2.4 million citizens of metropolitan Toronto had been represented by 106 councillors. After amalgamation they would be represented by just 45 members of city council. As a result, citizens would have less access to their councillors and would find it difficult to have input on local issues.

Among those opposed to the plan was John Sewell, a former Toronto mayor and a passionate community organizer. With an initial group of 22, Sewell formed Citizens for

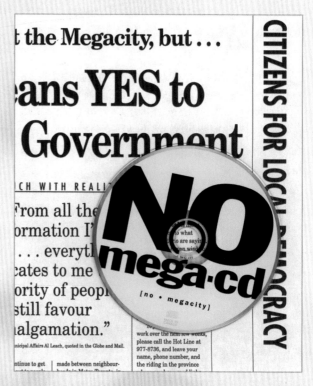

Local Democracy (C4LD). Through meetings, a newsletter, media announcements, a Web site, and a CD titled *No Mega-CD*, C4LD gathered support. Of the 500 deputations (presentations) made during public hearings on the plan, 90 per cent opposed amalgamation. In March, 1997, six local municipal governments organized referendums on the issue. A majority of 76 per cent voted against amalgamation.

Despite the referendum results, the provincial government went ahead, and Toronto became an amalgamated city on January 1, 1998. The government did, however, make some changes to its plans. C4LD lost its battle, but succeeded in exercising the rights of citizens in a democracy by giving a voice to people who opposed government policy. It also demonstrated the power of new forms of communication, such as the Internet, in spreading information quickly to many people.

Elected and Appointed Municipal Officials

All adult Canadian citizens who reside in the municipality (or own or rent land in it), or are married to someone who does, may vote in municipal elections and run for municipal office. The people elected form a **municipal council**. Municipal councils, whether urban or rural, vary in size but generally have fewer members than provincial and federal levels of government. Heads of councils, called mayors or reeves, are usually elected by a general vote. Other members of council, called councillors or aldermen, are elected in one of two ways.

A municipality may have an at-large system with a general vote, so that candidates who receive the most votes are elected. Alternatively, the municipality may be divided into geographic subdivisions, or **wards**, with a number of councillors running in each ward. In this system, voters are restricted to voting for candidates in their own ward. Most cities are organized on the basis of ward elections, while most towns and almost all townships and villages hold at-large elections. Some municipalities combine systems, electing councillors in wards and mayors-at-large.

municipal council: The group of people elected to govern on local issues. The head of the council is called the mayor or reeve. Other members are called councillors or aldermen.

ward: A geographic subdivision, often encompassing a neighbourhood or several neighbourhoods, which is used as the designation for an elected councillor.

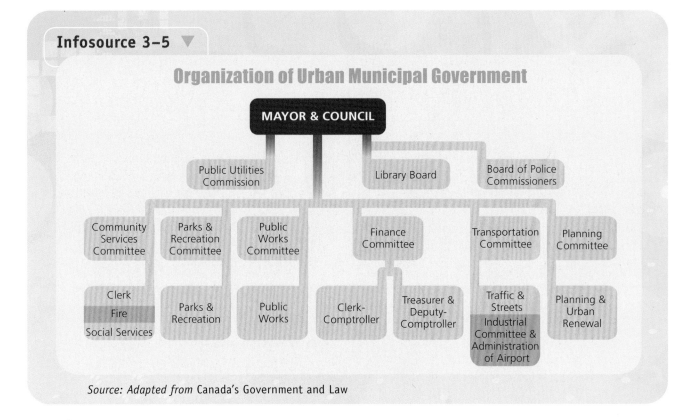

Infosource 3–5 ▼

Organization of Urban Municipal Government

MAYOR & COUNCIL

- Public Utilities Commission
- Library Board
- Board of Police Commissioners

- Community Services Committee
- Parks & Recreation Committee
- Public Works Committee
- Finance Committee
- Transportation Committee
- Planning Committee

- Clerk
- Fire
- Social Services
- Parks & Recreation
- Public Works
- Clerk-Comptroller
- Treasurer & Deputy-Comptroller
- Traffic & Streets
- Industrial Committee & Administration of Airport
- Planning & Urban Renewal

Source: Adapted from Canada's Government and Law

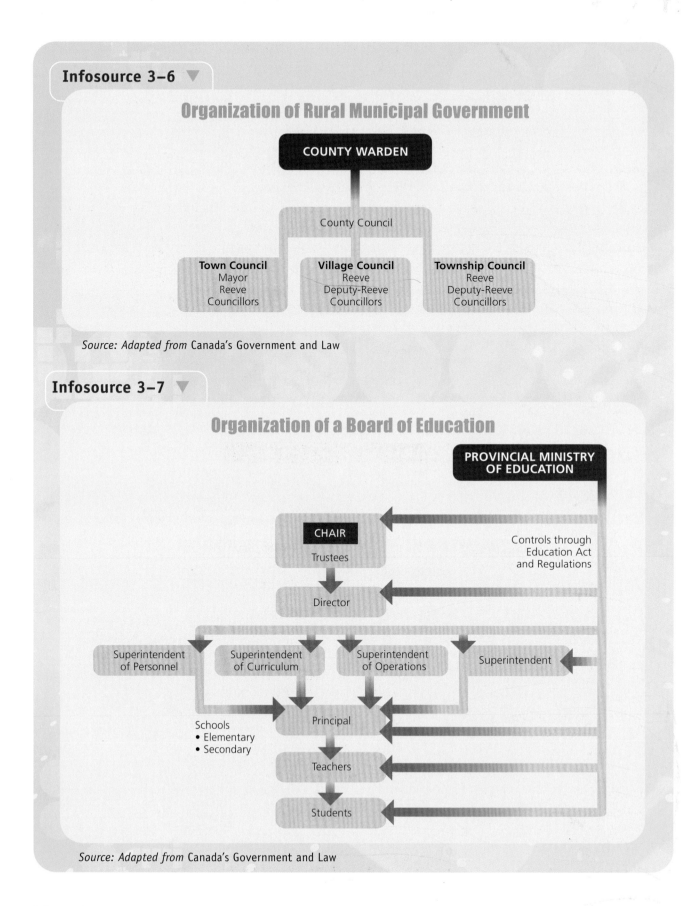

Organization of Rural Municipal Government

COUNTY WARDEN

County Council

Town Council	**Village Council**	**Township Council**
Mayor	Reeve	Reeve
Reeve	Deputy-Reeve	Deputy-Reeve
Councillors	Councillors	Councillors

Source: Adapted from Canada's Government and Law

Organization of a Board of Education

PROVINCIAL MINISTRY OF EDUCATION

Controls through Education Act and Regulations

CHAIR

Trustees

Director

Superintendent of Personnel

Superintendent of Curriculum

Superintendent of Operations

Superintendent

Schools
• Elementary
• Secondary

Principal

Teachers

Students

Source: Adapted from Canada's Government and Law

Municipal elections serve to elect people not only to councils, but also to other bodies, such as **school boards** and public utility commissions (regulators of electricity, natural gas, and other natural resources). Members of advisory committees, such as library boards or parks commissions, are usually appointed. The wide range of issues dealt with by local governments and the small number of councillors make these boards and committees influential decision makers in a community.

In urban areas, much of the work of local government is handled by the **civil service**. This is made up of people who are hired, not elected. Departments carry out the delivery of services. Department managers, the senior civil servants of local government, are responsible for the actions of their departments. For example, residents might contact a civil servant — the recreation director, for example — rather than an elected councillor about a broken bench in a park. Similarly, while trustees (the school board's elected officials) often receive calls from parents, more often it is the senior civil servants who work for the board — for example, school principals, superintendents, or even the director of education — who hear citizens' concerns.

school board: Group of people elected to make decisions about schools in a particular area.

civil service: Network of people hired to work for the government. In local government, they run the municipal departments that provide local services. Also called public service.

ACTIVITIES THE INQUIRING CITIZEN

BE Informed

1. Compare urban municipal government with rural municipal government (see Infosources 3–5 and 3–6).

2. Why have some municipalities amalgamated?

3. Examine the cartoon on page 76.
   a) What does it show?
   b) What message does the cartoonist present?
   c) Does the cartoon convey its message effectively? Explain.

BE Purposeful

4. Prepare an information booklet for your municipality. Include:
   - a visual that illustrates its organization

   - the positions and names of the council members and their phone numbers
   - other bodies (e.g., school board), with names and phone numbers of their members
   - the key municipal departments that provide services, with phone numbers

BE Active

5. **a)** Work with a partner to interview a local government official. Ask about duties, powers, rewards, challenges, job qualifications, and term of office. Report your findings to the class.
   b) As a class, vote for the most interesting interviewee, and invite him or her to visit your class.

How Are Decisions Made at the Municipal Level?

Municipal government councillors and mayors (or reeves) make decisions on matters for which they are responsible. Their responsibilities include:

- seeing that services are delivered by various local departments, such as the Department of Parks and Recreation

Infosource 3–8 ▼

THE MUNICIPAL DECISION-MAKING PROCESS

Stage 1

Committees meet, review staff reports and public submissions, make recommendations, and prepare proposals. (Members of the public may make presentations, called deputations, related to any item on the committee's agenda. In Ontario, all committee and council meetings must be open to the public, with very few exceptions.)

Stage 2

Items to be discussed at council are outlined on an agenda. Various background reports, including committee reports, items of correspondence, and other materials, are given to members.

Stage 3

Council meeting, presided over by the mayor or reeve, is called. (It is open to the public.)
- Formal proposals (known as motions) must be supported by at least one other member (seconded) before being discussed.
- Council members debate motions.
- Municipal bylaws must be considered three times (three readings) before being voted on.
- Motions and bylaws usually pass by a simple majority vote.

Stage 4

Bylaws are signed by the clerk and the presiding officer, numbered, and affixed with the municipal seal.

Stage 5

Bylaws take effect.

- creating policies and passing **bylaws** on issues, such as whether to put a stop sign on your street
- planning for the future, called **local planning**, such as land development

Municipal councils often organize committees that are responsible for different services. For example, a municipality might have committees for transportation, public works (sewage, water, and garbage services), and parks and recreation. Each committee examines issues in its area of responsibility and then makes recommendations on which the council votes.

Each official municipal decision is the result of a process that includes several stages, as shown in Infosource 3–8.

bylaw: Regulation passed by municipal councils. Provincial governments can review and overturn this legal decision.

local planning: Municipal responsibility for forming policies and procedures for the future.

Bylaws — such as regulations for unleashed dogs — are a local responsibility.

ACTIVITIES   THE INQUIRING CITIZEN

BE Informed

1. What is a bylaw? How could a bylaw that requires dogs to be on a leash promote the common good?

BE Purposeful

2. Why do you think that motions must be supported by at least two councillors before being discussed? Do you think this is fair?

3. Review Infosource 3–8. How is this decision-making process similar to, or different from, the process described in Chapter 1 (page 15)?

BE Active

4. **a)** Track a recent decision that was made by your local government about a specific issue. Explain briefly what happened at each stage of the decision-making process.
   b) To what extent do you think the decision was made democratically? Explain.

How Can You Participate at the Local Level?

For democracy to work, people must participate and their opinions must be valued. This is particularly true at the local level, since this is where people have the greatest opportunity to voice their views and influence community decisions. Citizen participation benefits not only the people and the community, but also the decision-making process. Here are the reasons why.

Community participation is beneficial because:

- Citizens are most aware of their own needs, community problems, and available resources.
- Community organizations have more access to local information and local history.
- Citizens have most at stake. Commitment to a solution is greater and the chances of its success are strengthened when those who must live with the outcome are involved in making the decision.
- Programs and services are more appropriate, efficient, and effective.

Decision making in local government usually includes a stage for public input. There are several ways in which citizens can express their views:

- Municipal governments hold public consultations — meetings or surveys to find out what citizens think about a particular problem or proposal. Citizens can attend meetings to express their views.
- Citizens can be appointed to sit on municipal boards, commissions, and advisory councils.
- Individuals can get involved in local elections by working on a campaign.
- Individuals can run for elected office and vote for the candidates they prefer.

Expressing Your Views at the Local Level

As a citizen or a member of a community group, you can express your views in various ways. Many people participate locally without ever involving formal authorities. Involvement in social action activities in your school — such as an AIDS Awareness campaign, peer conflict resolution, Earth Week, a play that challenges stereotypes about street youth, or fundraising for a battered women's shelter — is an example of local participation. At the local level, even one person working alone can make an impact on the quality of life in the community — especially if she or he takes a leadership role.

We have all heard the phrase, "There is strength in numbers." When individuals collaborate and convince other local citizens to work with them, it is called **grassroots organizing**. The most effective opportunity for citizens to participate in the local decision-making process is when they work together. As a group, individuals with common goals can effectively research an issue, decide on a strategy, and set up a plan of action. Grassroots organizations often participate in civil society by educating the public, fundraising, providing services for needy groups, demonstrating, working for candidates in elections, and building links with other grassroots groups. Whether they are members of a neighbourhood or like-minded students in a high school class, a grassroots group can present forceful arguments and effective strategies to influence local government.

grassroots organizing:
Organizing society at the local level, as distinguished from the centres of political leadership.

Grassroots organizations get involved in a wide range of community issues.

Contacting Your Municipal Officials

Some issues may require the involvement of a local representative. The job of a municipal representative is to protect the public interests — that is, the needs and wishes of the people they represent. If you have a problem that you wish to discuss with your municipal councillor, your school board trustee, or even the mayor, you will likely find him or her much easier to reach than your provincial or federal representative.

Infosource 3-9 ▼

How to Participate in Local Government: Starting Points

Collect signatures on a petition advocating a course of action you would like to see followed.

Begin taking action individually or as a group.

Visit a local politician and discuss your views. Get government officials involved in your issue.

Attend a council or board meeting and make a deputation.

Write a letter to your municipal council. Get others who share your opinions to do so as well.

Graham L. Downey
Municipal Councillor, City of Halifax

Graham L. Downey has been a municipal councillor in Halifax for 26 years. During that time, he has been deputy mayor and has participated on numerous city boards and commissions. He represents downtown Halifax, where he has lived all his life.

Q: Why did you become involved in municipal politics?

A: I always felt I wanted to do something in the community. The area where I lived was going through major changes. There were a lot of derelict buildings and houses boarded up. I thought I could do something to help improve the neighbourhood. When I became councillor, we got some federal help through the neighbourhood improvement programs. Now you see nice trees through the streets. It's a real mix of people who live here — low and middle income families, professionals, children, seniors.

Q: Are you in close contact with your constituents?

A: My family has its roots in the history of Halifax and we're like an anchor in the community. I was involved in sports and groups coming up all through childhood. Later, my brother and I owned a club, and everybody came to hear the musicians we brought in from Toronto and New York. And now, because I've been a councillor for a long time, people know me. They know that if they call me, they don't get a machine, they get me. My line is always open and I do whatever I can for the community.

Q: Why is that contact important?

A: As a municipal councillor, you're the people's man. You're closer to the people than if you were a federal or provincial representative. For instance, a woman called yesterday about an older gentleman in her co-op building whose stove had been cut off. She and her neighbours were worried about him and that he might start a fire by accident. I got hold of the gentleman, called him personally. I made sure the stove was turned back on. That kind of individual attention is an important part of the job.

Q: What role has community involvement played in your life?

A: Community involvement has been a great experience and even an education for me. I only had my grade 7 schooling because I had to go out and work when I was young. I did a lot of my own schooling, going to night school. Then through my work as a stage hand at the CBC, and as a politician and club owner, I met all sorts of people. You don't realize that you are learning as you meet people by just being around them. As a young person, it's important to be involved. Experience is always there for you, if you want it. It's a great way to learn and to develop yourself. If you want to learn something, get involved.

Municipal politicians are elected to serve community interests and resolve community problems. They generally live in the community they represent. As residents of the community, they are aware of local conditions and issues. A good municipal representative should be accessible, willing to listen to his or her constituents' views, and ready to act on their wishes.

Whether the issue is parking on your street or a threatened closing of your community centre, there are numerous ways for you to make your views known through the right channels.

ACTIVITIES THE INQUIRING CITIZEN

BE Informed

1. **a)** According to the text, what are the benefits of participating in your community? Explain in your own words.
   b) What other benefits could you add to the list?

2. What is meant by "grassroots organizing"?

3. **a)** Review the photographs on page 85. Explain what is happening in each one.
   M b) Using newspapers and magazines, find three additional photographs that show citizens participating in their communities.

BE Purposeful

4. **a)** In what ways might you be able to participate at the grassroots level?
   b) In what ways might you be able to participate in the local government decision-making process? Identify an issue and decide which of the methods shown in Infosource 3–9 might be appropriate.
   c) What might be the opportunities or challenges you might encounter if you did participate in either of these ways?

5. Graham Downey thinks of himself as "the people's man." What does he mean by this? Support your answer with evidence from the interview.

BE Active

6. Prepare a deputation to your local council related to an issue of interest to your class. You might wish to use an issue identified in activity 4 above. Make sure that the issue is a municipal one, and that you are well informed about all aspects of it. Carefully prepare a presentation outlining your view of the issue and what you think should be done. (See also the Citizen's Toolkit on page 99.)

Should School Boards Make Exclusive Soft-Drink Deals?

Sometimes local politicians make decisions that are not supported by the people they represent. When a large urban school board signed an exclusive million-dollar deal with the multinational Pepsi-Cola Corporation, many people became upset. Students, teachers, parents, and other members of the community exercised their democratic rights. This case study illustrates some of the strategies used by citizens to attempt to influence decision makers at the local level.

Infosource 3–10 ▼

Pepsi to Be Sold in Schools

The Toronto Board of Education has agreed to remove all competing vending machines from its schools by next month, giving Pepsi exclusive sales access to the student population. In exchange, Pepsi will pay the Board $1.14 million over the next three years.

Sandra Bussin, a trustee of the board, said the money generated by the exclusive contract will help sustain services like lunch programs. "It's not a happy decision to make, but these aren't happy times." Under the agreement, Pepsi will install pop and juice vending machines in all secondary and senior schools, and juice vending machines in all junior and primary schools. Other promotional opportunities include the distribution of Pepsi-sponsored videos in schools.

Most of the money generated by the deal will go toward the board's cafeteria operations, which are running at a deficit.

Source: Adapted from Globe and Mail

Infosource 3–11 ▼

Protestors Express Their Views

Chanting and screaming and clutching "students are not for sale" signs, a group of about 50 students demonstrated in front of the Toronto Board of Education building and then filed into the lobby. The protestors then joined a committee meeting, waiting more than two hours for a chance to make deputations to trustees. Their presentations lasted another two emotionally charged hours.

Source: Adapted from Toronto Star

PUBLIC OPINION ON THE SOFT-DRINK AGREEMENT

There were 36 deputations presented to the school board on this issue. Only one deputant spoke in favour. The following is a sample of what was presented.

Monica Prendergast, English teacher: The public education system operates on a number of ideal principles. One of the primary ones is that the school environment should, and indeed must function as a safe haven from the excesses and confusions of the speed and profit-driven consumer culture. Within our walls, students are people, not customers.

Shauna Richler-Laneit, student: I agree that we need to think of ways to solve the budgetary problem. The students would be more than willing to work with you guys on that. But if we start looking to a corporate answer every time we have a budgetary issue, then I don't even really need to paint the [future] picture of the schools I see.

Vanessa Henderson, student: As for the advertising, I think that Pepsi uses an unfair, empty-body image to endorse their products. The skinny models used in both Pepsi and Diet Pepsi ads are unrealistic and potentially harmful for the students they're aimed at…. Are these the reminders we want in schools? I know that the board must provide a safe learning environment. Does perpetuating the high rate of eating disorders constitute a safe policy? Obviously not.

George Shepherd, physical education teacher: The Pepsi deal opens the door to corporate sponsorship at the school level…. Individuals with connections will now be able to attract nothing but the best in athletic talent to their schools. That sense of [fair] competition, of which we so often speak, will be a thing of the past.

Donna Buck, parent: My first concern about Pepsi coming into the schools was because of [its] sugar content. But actually considering, I'm upset by it because of the caffeine content. Caffeine is a drug that affects peoples' moods [and] in fact makes [kids] jittery and nervous.

John Weatherup, local union leader: I'm president of Local 134 of CUPE [Canadian Union of Public Employees] representing the food service workers [and others]. I understand concern about bringing Pepsi into our schools. Sitting on the Food Service Committee that negotiated this deal, we were not trying to sell anybody down the river. But we have women in the Food Service Department — a 100 of them — who are afraid they're going to lose their jobs. I don't like Pepsi in general. But in fact for the Board of Education and the women in [cafeteria services] it's their livelihood.

Source: Adapted from transcripts, Toronto Board of Education

In spite of the strong deputations against the Pepsi deal, the Toronto Board of Education went ahead with it in 1994. A few years later, when the deal came up for renewal, Pepsi lost out to the Coca Cola Company. Coca Cola's contract with the amalgamated Toronto District School Board, similar to the one made with Pepsi, took effect on January 1, 2000.

ANALYZING THE ISSUE

BE Purposeful

1. In your own words, explain the issue in this case.

2. **a)** What is the main argument in favour of the deal with Pepsi?
   b) List at least three arguments against the deal, given in the text.
   c) Which arguments do you find the most persuasive? Which do you find the least persuasive? Why?

3. **a)** What was the final decision in the Pepsi case?
   b) Did this decision reflect the wishes of the public? Explain.

4. **a)** The Toronto Board went ahead with the Pepsi deal despite opposition. Do you think it should have done so? Give reasons for your view.

   b) How do you think public decisions should be made when members of the public do not agree on what best serves the common good?

5. What point is made in the cartoon above? How does the cartoon connect with the soft-drink deal? Do you think the point is made effectively? Why or why not?

BE Active

6. Work with a partner. Role-play a discussion between a student opposed to the Pepsi deal and a school trustee who voted in favour of the deal. Use the arguments found in Infosources 3–10, 3–11, and 3–12, as well as your own opinions.

Recognizing Point of View

A **point of view** is a position someone takes in expressing his or her observation of an event, situation, idea, or issue. This position is often supported with reasons and facts, but a person's point of view is also influenced by many personal factors. For example, age, gender, family background, culture, religion, friends, and personal experiences can all play a part. As a result, people often view the same issue differently.

When people observe things from different points of view, what they report is likely to differ. Recognizing points of view can help you evaluate which information is most useful. When trying to recognize points of view, use these suggestions:

- Identify the subject being discussed, and the speaker.

- Identify which aspects of the subject are emphasized by the speaker.

- Identify any aspects of the subject that are downplayed by the speaker.

- Based on what you have identified in the steps above, describe the speaker's point of view.

Putting It Into Practice

1. Using the steps above, determine the point of view of each speaker in Infosource 3–12.

2. Compare your responses with a partner.

3. As a class, discuss the following questions: Why can it be difficult to recognize point of view? What additional information would you need to understand each speaker's point of view better? Why is it important for citizens to recognize other people's points of view?

FOCUS ON AN ISSUE

Can Citizens Influence Planning Decisions?

Municipal governments are responsible for making decisions to resolve conflicts within the community. One area in which conflicts often arise is land use and development. It is not surprising that citizens often have a lot to say about plans for how the land around their homes will be used. Conflicts about planning — or the way in which land will be used — create some very emotional debates.

While the public is asked to participate in planning issues, citizens are sometimes left wondering if the politicians and planners have really listened to them at all. The fight over the Mitchell Mansion, a historic building in Halifax, Nova Scotia, was one such case.

Look back at Infosource 2–12, Different Degrees of Participation (page 64). Where would this example of participation fall on the scale?

"We really value community participation when making decisions. Plan 1 is too expensive. Plan 2 will take too long. Now which plan do you prefer?"

The Mitchell Mansion was built in the 1870s on about two hectares of land. Local citizens considered it a beautiful and unique landmark in their neighbourhood. They were prepared to fight to protect it. In the 1970s and 1980s, the citizens participated in drawing up a Municipal Development Plan. They stated strongly that the kind of development they favoured in the area was low-rise housing around the mansion. The following timeline shows the decisions and actions that followed.

Infosource 3–13 ▼ **TIMELINE OF MITCHELL MANSION**

February 1987

The estate of the late Colonel Mitchell asks Halifax City Council to change official plans and allow high-rise development on the land where the old house is located.

Halifax's Planning Department rejects the request.

February/March 1987

Citizens hold a meeting to stop high-rise development and to save the mansion.

April 1987

Halifax council upholds the official Municipal Development Plan, initially rejecting the request to allow high-rise development on the Mitchell property.

Summer 1987

Concerned Citizens for the Mitchell Property (CCMP) is formed to save the old house from being torn down.

Fall 1987

CCMP attempts to buy the house, intending to convert it into a museum. The estate refuses to sell.

December 3, 1987

City Hall issues a permit, allowing the owners to demolish the house.

December 7, 1987

CCMP holds a petition drive and protests in front of the house.

March 1988

The mayor delays demolition for 30 days.

CCMP prints 3000 pamphlets and plans a letter-writing campaign.

April 1988

Mitchell house is torn down.

Source: Adapted from The Drama of Democracy

One year after the mansion was demolished, the owners of the Mitchell property applied for rezoning of their land to allow high-rise building. The Halifax Council suddenly ended its policy of sharing documents with citizens at least two days before a public meeting. Instead, citizens were allowed to view documents only two hours before the meetings. Citizens protested this change in policy and the Planning Advisory Committee of the council recommended that the rezoning proposal be rejected. Meanwhile, the owners of the Mitchell property gathered 255 signatures on their own petition requesting rezoning. Rezoning was approved by city council.

The Mitchell Mansion after demolition

Contrasting Views of Democracy

Citizen: I really think that democratic principles were violated in this case…. Democracy is not ideal, but it's better than anything else. There have to be checks and balances in the system, but I feel there won't be any until we get a stronger council to give direction to staff…. [I]f a group has ultimate power, then it won't use it wisely. We have to protect democracy.

Developer: I get angry when I hear the opponents of a project say, "If this is a democracy, then elected representatives have to listen to us the people and refuse this." A democracy has to respect and represent the rights of individuals too. We have to balance the rights of the individual and the community — that's what democracy has to mean.

Council Member: We're democratic. We say that if a man owns property, he's entitled to do something with it. That's where the system falls apart from the citizen's point of view because the ordinary citizen is left unprotected. When he buys a piece of property he has no guarantee that his neighbourhood won't change. I'd like to stop that. It's time we had some security.

Source: Halifax Council public hearing. *Quoted in* The Drama of Democracy

Newspaper Editorial

Once again Halifax City Hall has demonstrated its weak vision of grassroots democracy. Earlier this year, [municipal] council ended its policy of releasing relevant staff reports and other documents two or three days in advance of public meetings…. With the documents safely out of public view until the last moment, they need not worry about being embarrassed by citizens or reporters…. After six months [of negotiations between staff and developers], the public will see the application two hours before it comes up. The romantics among us like to think of civic politics as the root of democracy, but this action is barely worthy of [a democratic society].

Source: Halifax Daily News

ANALYZING THE ISSUE

BE Informed

1. Examine Infosource 3–13.
   a) What were the owners of the Mitchell estate asking the planning department and city council to do in February 1987?
   b) Why did this concern local residents?
   c) What did the local residents do to try to save Mitchell House?
   d) How did the local government respond?
   e) What was the eventual outcome?

BE Purposeful

2. Review Infosource 3–14.
   a) Describe each person's point of view.
   b) In this case it appears that the rights of individuals (the property owners) won over the goals of the community. Why do you think this was so?

3. Sometimes municipalities protect and preserve historical buildings by declaring them "heritage buildings." These buildings cannot be altered in any significant way without the approval of city council. The Halifax City Council was unwilling to make the Mitchell Mansion a heritage building against the owner's wishes. Why was this the case? Why was it an important issue?

BE Active

4. Imagine that you are a reporter for a Halifax newspaper. Write a brief editorial that gives your opinion of how the decision was made to demolish Mitchell Mansion. Was it democratic? Was it fair? Use specific evidence to support your view. Alternatively, present your view of the case in the form of a cartoon.

What Are the Challenges for Municipal Government?

If you have ever wondered why there aren't more parks in your community, or been crammed into a jam-packed city bus, or worried that your family wouldn't be able to find an affordable place to live in the city, you have experienced some of the problems of mass urbanization — the enormous increase in city populations. Mass urbanization has created new problems in traffic, recreation, health care, welfare, housing, and the safety of citizens and their property. Municipal governments must address these new pressures by providing new services. And these services are all expensive.

Today, if you want access to ice arenas or a quicker ride to work using public transit, your local government may ask you to pay a greater portion of the cost of those services. Municipal governments have two basic choices: they can provide fewer services or they can generate more money to pay for the services. Some governments have made a third choice, which is to reduce some services and charge more money for others.

These are only a few local issues currently facing municipal governments. Other important municipal challenges — all of which require major funding — include:

- increased waste
- subsidized public housing
- child care
- welfare
- urban renewal
- child poverty
- crime
- homelessness

Who pays for garbage collection? What happens when the cost of garbage collection goes up?

In the past, provinces have contributed large grants to local governments for local services. Today, as provinces try to curb their spending, these grants have shrunk. While the demand for local services has increased, the provincial commitment to support these local services has decreased. Municipal governments are caught in a squeeze between rising costs and shrinking resources.

Which municipal government challenge does the following newspaper article describe? What suggestion does the mayor of Toronto make to help alleviate this problem? Why do you think he makes this suggestion?

Infosource 3–16 ▼

Mayor Pleads for Funds

The mayor of Toronto has formally advised both Queen's Park [the provincial government] and Ottawa [the federal government] that the city can no longer cope with its homeless crisis and is in desperate need of increased provincial and federal funding…. Mayor Mel Lastman, who released his letters to the media yesterday, said that a shortage of money from the other levels of government is cause for grave concern…. In his correspondence to Ontario's premier Mike Harris, Mayor Lastman urged him to contribute more of the share of providing for the estimated 27 000 people who use homeless services in the city.

Source: Adapted from National Post

These people are protesting the increasing problem of homelessness in Toronto. What is the message they are trying to convey?

Analyzing an Issue

Where do you stand on the challenges facing your community? How can you analyze the issues and decide what you think should be done?

1. Explore the issue.
- Learn as much as you can about it in newspapers and magazines, on the Internet, and using other community resources.
- State the issue clearly.
- Ask questions about what you have learned.
- Identify the points of view of other concerned citizens.

2. Consider the options.
- Identify the different courses of action that could be followed to resolve the issue.
- Predict what might happen in each case.
- Identify the best options, keeping in mind the differing viewpoints of all concerned.

3. Make a decision.
- Rank the options you have identified.
- Choose the best option, and justify your choice with reasons and evidence.

4. Take action (where appropriate).
- Share your conclusions with others in your group or community.
- Decide what action is appropriate.

Putting It Into Practice

1. From your local newspaper, find a story about an issue that is currently being debated in your community.

2. Use the steps above to analyze the issue. Present your conclusions to the class.

A Special Challenge: Aboriginal Self-Government

For thousands of years before Europeans settled in Canada, Aboriginal Nations had their own government systems. In Chapter 1, you read about one system used by the Iroquois Confederacy. In recent decades, Aboriginal Nations have been arguing for the right to govern themselves once again. Many have been negotiating with the federal and provincial governments to establish self-government in certain areas.

There has been much discussion about what exactly is meant by Aboriginal self-government. In general terms, it means that matters directly affecting the daily life of Aboriginal people will be under their control. These matters include education, language, culture, and the development or control of land, water, and other resources. Aboriginal governments would not have jurisdiction over relationships with other countries or the creation of armies, currency, or postal services. These matters would remain a federal responsibility.

In some ways, Aboriginal self-government will be similar to the provincial level, which deals with matters such as education and culture. However, Aboriginal self-government is sometimes compared with the municipal level because it will address issues that are closest to the community. Decisions will be made by people who belong to the community. In that way, Aboriginal people believe, they will be able to address their own needs more effectively than the federal government has been able to do.

Aboriginal people believe that their right to govern themselves is inherent — that is, a right they have always had.

Limited Powers of Municipal Governments

In each Province the legislature may exclusively make laws in relation [to]…local works and undertakings.

— *Section 92, Constitution Act, 1867*

Municipal governments sometimes find it difficult to solve the issues they face, because they do not exist in the constitution as a separate level of authority. Municipal governments only have as much authority as provincial legislatures will give them. Sometimes school boards and local governments are unable to respond to citizen concerns because of these limits. The provinces — which created the municipalities and provide a significant share of their funding — place restrictions on how much local governments can do. For example, a city may want to provide its police officers with more powerful weapons, but provincial Police Acts may prevent this.

In some cases, municipal governments have neither the authority nor the finances to carry out their responsibilities. Unlike provinces, cities and towns are not allowed to go into debt. This often means, since they are unable to raise property taxes, they cannot start new programs unless the province approves — and pays. For example, a city might need to provide more shelters for the homeless. However, if the provincial government refuses to allow an increase in property taxes, the city may not be able to afford to build the shelters. On the other hand, a local school board may not feel it can afford a new program, but may be forced by provincial legislation to provide it.

> **Did You Know?**
>
> If the federal government raises income taxes or the province increases the sales tax, you have no recourse. However, citizens may appeal some municipal decisions to the provincial government. For example, if your municipal government increases your home's assessment (the value placed on your property for tax purposes), you can request the province to review that decision.

Without approval from the provincial government, a municipality cannot increase taxes to provide services, even if the residents are willing to pay.

What are the solutions to all these challenges? In 1990, the Federation of Canadian Municipalities suggested that the Canadian constitution needed to be amended to keep up with the changes in society. They argued that, since municipalities carry the largest burden of services, they should be recognized as a separate form of government with accompanying powers, including the right to a larger share of tax revenue.

Others feel that complex local services require more financial support from the other two levels of government. Local governments should work harder with federal and provincial governments to share expenses. Co-operation among the three governments is necessary to provide services for the needs of all Canadians. What is needed, they argue, is a new agreement among municipal, provincial, and federal governments on the sharing of power and costs.

ACTIVITIES   THE INQUIRING CITIZEN

BE Informed

1. Find evidence in the text to support the following statements.
   - Municipalities face many challenges today.
   - It is difficult for municipal governments to find solutions to their problems because they are limited in terms of money and authority to make certain changes.

2. a) What is the purpose of Aboriginal self-government?
   b) In what ways is Aboriginal self-government similar to municipal government?

BE Purposeful

3. Review Infosource 3–16.
   a) What is the problem identified in the article? What is the mayor requesting?
   b) What suggestions would you make to the mayor with regard to the problem?

BE Active

4. a) Interview teenagers, adults, and local councillors to compile a list of what they see to be the primary challenges facing your municipal government.
   b) Investigate what steps, if any, your municipality is taking to deal with these challenges.

5. Assume that you have been asked to serve on a Youth Task Force to study the problems in the way local government services are provided in your community. You will present your findings to the Federation of Canadian Municipalities, which is looking for ways to deal with the many challenges faced by municipal governments. Work with a group to prepare three recommendations.

BE Informed

1. Use each of the following terms in a sentence, taking care to show how the term is connected to citizenship at the local level.
   a) municipality
   b) bylaws
   c) school board
   d) grassroots organizing
   e) essential services
   f) amalgamation

2. Create a collage of newspaper headlines that shows services offered at the local level in your community. If possible, include some of the challenges faced by your municipal government.

BE Purposeful

3. a) Design an advertisement to explain to residents of your community why it is important for them to know about and participate in civic issues. If you prefer, you might wish to encourage them to join a particular organization that is interested in civic issues. Consider one of the following formats: a 30-second radio commercial, a public transit poster, or a button. Be sure to choose a specific audience before you design your advertisement.
   b) Write a paragraph that explains your advertisement.

4. Work with a partner or group to investigate the contributions made by one individual or one group to your community. Choose a person or group that has been involved with issues of local importance for a long time. Find out about relevant issues, decisions, and actions. What beliefs and values were expressed through these actions? What were some of the conflicting interests, and how were they resolved? If possible, interview your subject or members of the group you have chosen, and make a five-minute video of your interview.

BE Active

5. Many schools and school boards have formed partnerships with businesses, corporations, and other groups. Find out about partnerships that your school or school board has made. What is the purpose of the partnership? Can the partnership affect what is taught in the school? Why or why not? Contact your student council, the chair of your school council, or your principal to obtain information.

6. Conduct your own Student Town Council meeting.
   a) To prepare:
   ■ Review the decision-making process for local government as shown in Infosource 3–8.
   ■ Attend a real council meeting. Pay particular attention to the roles played by councillors and department heads who might be present.

   b) Some students should choose roles as student mayor, student councillor, and student department heads. These students should prepare proposals of special interest to your class to discuss at a council meeting.
   c) Hold a Student Town Council meeting, at which you introduce, debate, and vote on your proposals for the town.
   d) Students who are not part of the council should serve as members of local organizations with an interest in the issue, reporters who will file stories with the local press, and a TV crew covering the event for a local community station.
   e) If possible, take action to implement the proposals you have passed.

4

Provincial and Federal Governments:

Building Your Knowledge

FOCUS YOUR LEARNING

The Informed Citizen

How are Canada's federal and provincial governments organized?

How do we choose the people who represent us in our governments?

What role do political parties play?

The Purposeful Citizen

Do our provincial and federal governments represent us effectively?

How democratic is our system of decision making at this level?

The Active Citizen

How can citizens use their vote wisely?

How can citizens voice their views to provincial and federal governments?

Our provincial and federal governments make decisions about many issues: education, pollution, unemployment, health care, and military spending, to name just a few. Sometimes these decisions are controversial. Think about smoking, cigarettes, government regulations. The words alone provoke strong reactions from Canadians of all ages.

Our provincial and federal governments have developed structures and processes that allow them to make decisions on difficult issues such as smoking regulations. In this chapter, you will explore some of these structures and processes. You will look at the way we choose the representatives who will make these decisions. And you will reflect on the roles and responsibilities of people like you.

Key Terms

- executive branch
- prime minister
- public or civil service
- legislative branch
- Leader of the Opposition
- bill
- judicial branch
- riding
- political party
- first past the post (FPTP)

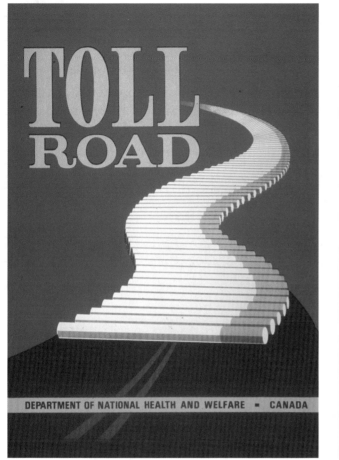

TOLL ROAD

DEPARTMENT OF NATIONAL HEALTH AND WELFARE ■ CANADA

IT MIGHT BE DIFFERENT

if you had nine lives!

DEPARTMENT OF NATIONAL HEALTH AND WELFARE, OTTAWA

WHAT DO **YOU** THINK?

Governments must address difficult issues on behalf of citizens. Yet citizens themselves often have strong and opposing views about what should be done. In recent years, for example, provincial governments have passed laws prohibiting smoking in public places. Governments have taken these steps to protect the health of the country's citizens. Yet there are many critics. For example, restaurant owners, people who legally sell tobacco products, many (but by no means all) smokers, and even some non-smokers argue that the laws restrict the freedoms of law-abiding citizens and infringe on the rights of smokers.

■ Examine the posters above. What is the message of each one? What is your reaction to the posters?

■ Critics of government regulations restricting smoking say that the rights of non-smokers are being given more importance than those of smokers. What are the rights of the majority on this issue? What are the rights of the minority? Should smoking be a "right"?

■ What effects might restricting smoking have on health care costs?

■ Does the government, in your view, have the right to restrict smoking? Why or why not?

What Makes Governments Act?

Why does a government make a decision like banning smoking in public places? As you saw in Chapter 2, our governments have a range of responsibilities, outlined in our constitution. They also act for other reasons, as shown below.

Infosource 4–1 ▼

GOVERNMENTS ACT BECAUSE OF...

CHANGING CIRCUMSTANCES
- Politicians and other government officials constantly monitor existing laws. If they see that a particular law or policy could be improved, they may propose changes.

ELECTION PROMISES
- When politicians run in elections, they and their parties promise to put certain plans into action. These plans are known as party platforms. The party that wins the election, and becomes the government, will try to put these plans into effect.

"If I win, I promise to..."

PUBLIC OPINION
- Sometimes the public will pressure governments to make a change following some spectacular event. For example, a particularly violent crime by a teenager may lead to calls for stiffer penalties for young offenders.
- Often public opinion builds up slowly. For example, the ban on smoking in public places was partly the result of growing public awareness about the dangers of smoking and second-hand smoke.
- Sometimes pressure comes from a particular group. For example, public health groups pressured governments to impose restrictions on smoking.

COURT DECISIONS
- Sometimes decisions made by courts cause governments to create or change laws.

How Are Our Federal and Provincial Governments Organized?

Our federal and provincial governments are organized into three branches. Each branch has its own set of powers, as shown in Infosource 4–2. These branches of government have their roots in our constitution, our traditions, and our laws.

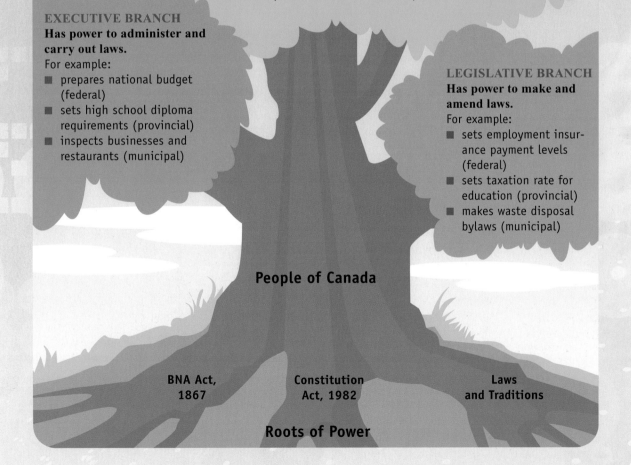

Infosource 4–2 ▼

THE THREE BRANCHES OF GOVERNMENT AND THE ROOTS OF POWER

JUDICIAL BRANCH
Has power to decide who has broken the law and to set penalties. Governments do not hold this power directly. Judges and courts at the federal and provincial levels hold the power.

EXECUTIVE BRANCH
Has power to administer and carry out laws.
For example:
- prepares national budget (federal)
- sets high school diploma requirements (provincial)
- inspects businesses and restaurants (municipal)

LEGISLATIVE BRANCH
Has power to make and amend laws.
For example:
- sets employment insurance payment levels (federal)
- sets taxation rate for education (provincial)
- makes waste disposal bylaws (municipal)

People of Canada

BNA Act, 1867

Constitution Act, 1982

Laws and Traditions

Roots of Power

What Is the Executive Branch?

executive branch: Branch of government that has the power to carry out the plans and policies of government.

The **executive branch** carries out the plans and policies of the government. At the federal level of government, the executive branch is made up of the prime minister, the cabinet (a group of government members with special responsibilities), and the public service (or civil service). At the provincial level, the executive branch is made up of the premier, the cabinet, and the provincial public service.

Canada's constitution declares that all laws are made in the name of the Queen, usually represented by the governor general (see Chapter 2). The prime minister, cabinet, and public service run the daily affairs of the federal government. Similarly, the lieutenant-governor is officially the Queen's representative at the provincial level, and the government is run by the premier, cabinet, and public servants.

Infosource 4–3 ▼

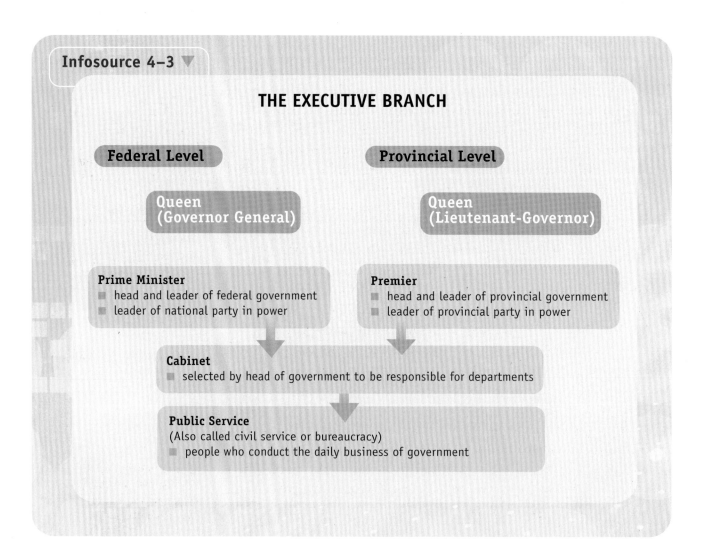

THE EXECUTIVE BRANCH

Federal Level

Queen (Governor General)

Prime Minister
- head and leader of federal government
- leader of national party in power

Provincial Level

Queen (Lieutenant-Governor)

Premier
- head and leader of provincial government
- leader of provincial party in power

Cabinet
- selected by head of government to be responsible for departments

Public Service
(Also called civil service or bureaucracy)
- people who conduct the daily business of government

The Federal Level: The Prime Minister

Canada's **prime minister** has many important roles.

- As leader of the nation, the prime minister speaks on behalf of all Canadians at national and international meetings. He or she addresses citizens on issues of national importance, and represents Canada on trips abroad. The prime minister also works with provincial premiers to make changes that will benefit Canadians.

- As head of the federal government, the prime minister recommends new judges and senators to be named by the governor general. Every four or five years, the prime minister asks the governor general to call an election.

- As leader of his or her political party, the prime minister acts as spokesperson for that party. The prime minister leads the **caucus**, the group of government members from his or her party.

A typical day in the working life of the prime minister is shown in Infosource 4–4.

The Cabinet

It is the job of the prime minister to choose members of the **cabinet**, the group that decides what the government policy should be. Usually, each cabinet member is given responsibility for one department of the government. Members of the cabinet are known as **ministers**. By tradition, cabinet members are elected members of Parliament, but in rare circumstances, senators and citizens who have not been elected can serve in the cabinet.

Cabinet ministers ask department staff to examine issues and draw up proposals for new laws in their area of responsibility. The ministers then introduce these proposals in the form of bills that might become laws. They speak on behalf of the department in public, and they are responsible for the department's budget.

Members of the cabinet work together, under the leadership of the prime minister, to discuss important decisions that the government must make. In cabinet meetings, ministers may express dissenting views and even question the leadership of the prime minister. In public, however, cabinet ministers are expected to show full support for the prime minister and the decisions of the government. This is known as **cabinet solidarity**. Cabinet ministers who are unable to support the decisions of the government publicly are expected to resign.

prime minister: The leader of the nation, head of the federal government, and leader of the party with the greatest number of seats in Parliament.

caucus: A group of representatives from the same political party in Parliament. Some people believe that the word "caucus" comes from the Algonquin word for "advisor."

cabinet: The group of ministers that decides what the government policy should be. Cabinet members usually have responsibility for particular departments of government, such as Foreign Affairs, Defence, and Justice.

minister: Member of the cabinet.

cabinet solidarity: The custom that cabinet members must appear united and in agreement with each other.

The prime minister has a demanding job, with a schedule that varies from day to day, according to issues and events. The prime minister takes a role as leader of the nation, leader of Parliament, leader of his or her political party, and leader of the cabinet. The following schedule shows just some aspects of the prime minister's job.

8:00 Spend an hour discussing national issues at a breakfast meeting with advisors.

9:00 Review the day's schedule with the chief of staff and executive assistant.

9:15 Meet with the Clerk of the Privy Council (Canada's top public servant) to review the agenda for the morning cabinet meeting.

9:45 Lead a weekly meeting of the Cabinet Committee on Priorities and Planning. Consult with group on important decisions. If issues to be discussed are controversial, debate sometimes continues through the lunch hour.

13:00 Meet with press secretary, who presents a brief on issues likely to be raised during the day's press interview.

13:25 Before entering the House of Commons, meet with policy advisors to discuss issues and events likely to be raised. Must be thoroughly prepared.

14:15 Along with cabinet ministers, respond to questions from opposition parties in the House of Commons (see page 113). Explain the government's stand on issues raised.

15:30 Meet with a journalist preparing an article on an upcoming meeting with world leaders.

16:30 Meet with cabinet ministers and government officials to discuss plans for a conference with provincial premiers.

17:30 Attend a reception for a group of business and labour leaders, make a short speech, and return to office.

18:15 Review documents and letters before going home for the evening. After supper, spend some time on family or personal matters.

21:00 Spend two hours reading documents before going to bed.

The official residence of Canada's prime minister is 24 Sussex Drive, in Ottawa.

The Public Service

Another part of the executive branch is the **public service**, also called the civil service or bureaucracy. As you saw in Chapter 3, public servants work to provide government services. They are employees of the government, and are not elected or chosen for their political beliefs. Public servants work in many jobs. They might gather statistics, write details for new laws, or research information to help in making new policies. They might collect taxes, process passports, deliver mail, check health regulations, and perform thousands of other tasks necessary for a government to run effectively.

Because public servants carry out the daily business of our nation, they have an important role. Many have the ability to influence how the government responds to the needs and requests of citizens. In fact, public servants are often the only direct contact that most citizens have with government.

public or civil service: The people hired to work for the government.

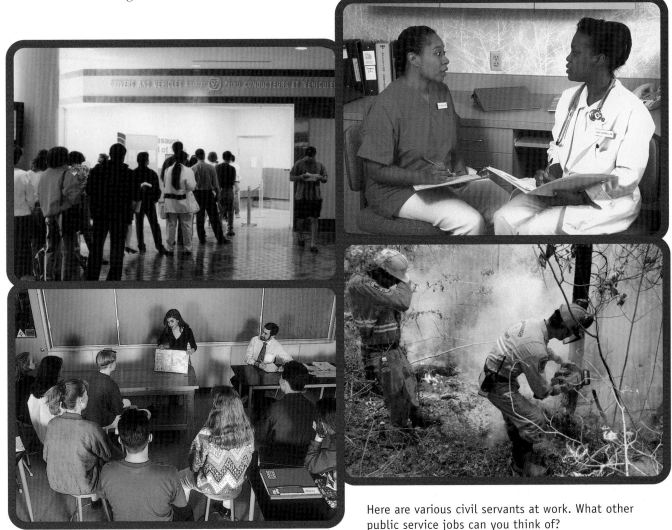

Here are various civil servants at work. What other public service jobs can you think of?

The Executive Branch at the Provincial Level

At the provincial level, the premier takes a leadership role similar to that of the prime minister. The premier asks the lieutenant-governor to call elections and name judges. He or she addresses the citizens of the province and works with other premiers and the federal government to defend the province's interests.

The premier chooses cabinet members to direct specific provincial affairs. These cabinet members are responsible for areas that fall under provincial jurisdiction (see Chapter 2). For example, they might include Ministers of Education, Municipal Affairs and Housing, Health, and Labour. In Ontario, the cabinet is sometimes referred to as the Executive Council.

Civil servants at the provincial level include police officers, education workers, and health care personnel.

ACTIVITIES   THE INQUIRING CITIZEN

BE Informed

1. Find three news articles that describe governments taking action. For each, explain which of the following is causing the government to act: changing circumstances, public opinion, court decisions, election promises.

2. a) Explain the role of the executive branch of government.
   b) Make a diagram of the executive branch at the federal level. Identify its main parts (e.g., cabinet) and the main duties of each part.

3. Review Infosource 4–4. Categorize the prime minister's activities according to the following roles: national leader, parliamentary leader, leader of a political party, cabinet leader.

4. Identify the jobs shown on page 111. Identify five other types of work performed by public servants at the provincial or federal level. Use the Blue Pages of your telephone directory.

BE Purposeful

5. a) What is "cabinet solidarity"? What is the purpose of cabinet solidarity?
   b) As a class, discuss some situations where a cabinet minister might not wish to follow cabinet solidarity.
   c) To what extent do you think elected representatives should follow cabinet solidarity?

6. Why are public servants not elected to their jobs? In your view, is this practice democratic?

BE Active

7. Prepare a job advertisement for the position of Canada's prime minister. Include a brief job description and personal qualities and experience you think are necessary for the job.

What Is the Legislative Branch?

The **legislative branch** of government is the branch that has the power to make and change laws. It is also called **Parliament**. The components of the legislative branch at the federal and provincial levels are shown in Infosource 4–5.

legislative branch: Branch of government that has the power to make, change, and repeal laws.

Parliament: The legislative branch of government.

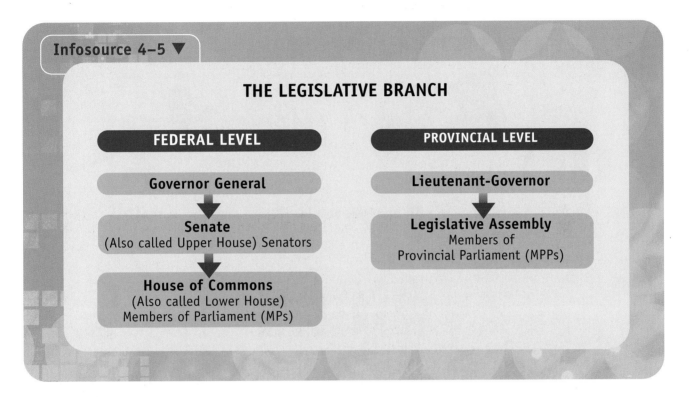

Infosource 4–5 ▼

THE LEGISLATIVE BRANCH

FEDERAL LEVEL

Governor General
↓
Senate
(Also called Upper House) Senators
↓
House of Commons
(Also called Lower House)
Members of Parliament (MPs)

PROVINCIAL LEVEL

Lieutenant-Governor
↓
Legislative Assembly
Members of
Provincial Parliament (MPPs)

The Federal Level: The House of Commons

The most powerful part of the legislative branch at the federal level is the House of Commons, in Ottawa. This is where elected representatives meet to discuss and vote on public issues. Representatives at the federal level are called **Members of Parliament** or **MPs**. The total number of "seats" (or places for members) in the House of Commons is determined by the population of Canada. As the population of Canada increases, so does the number of seats. In 2000, there were 301 seats in the House of Commons, up from 282 in 1984, and 295 in 1988.

MPs regularly discuss and debate issues and government policies. These debates are controlled by the Speaker of the House, who is also an elected member of Parliament. The Speaker is chosen by secret ballot by all the other MPs. He or she must then apply the rules of Parliament fairly and firmly to all members, including the prime minister.

Member of Parliament: Person chosen in elections to represent the citizens, and to debate and vote on public issues in Parliament.

Making and Changing Laws

bill: A written proposal for a law.

act: A written law passed by Parliament.

Parliament's main function is to make, change, or repeal (remove) laws in the areas given to it by our constitution. The written draft of a proposed law is called a **bill**. In order for a bill to become law, or an **act**, it must follow the procedure shown in Infosource 4–6.

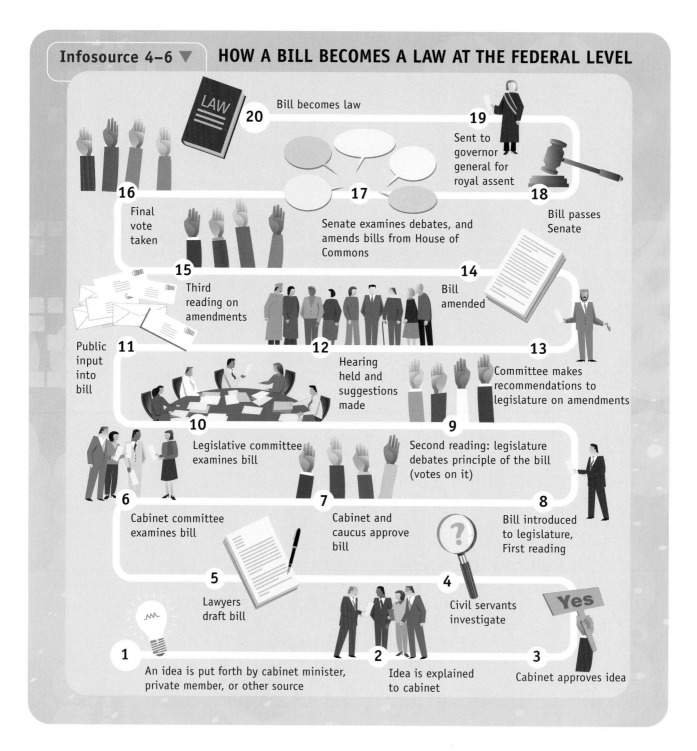

Infosource 4–6 ▼ **HOW A BILL BECOMES A LAW AT THE FEDERAL LEVEL**

20 Bill becomes law

19 Sent to governor general for royal assent

16 Final vote taken

17 Senate examines debates, and amends bills from House of Commons

18 Bill passes Senate

15 Third reading on amendments

14 Bill amended

11 Public input into bill

12 Hearing held and suggestions made

13 Committee makes recommendations to legislature on amendments

10 Legislative committee examines bill

9 Second reading: legislature debates principle of the bill (votes on it)

6 Cabinet committee examines bill

7 Cabinet and caucus approve bill

8 Bill introduced to legislature, First reading

5 Lawyers draft bill

4 Civil servants investigate

Yes

1 An idea is put forth by cabinet minister, private member, or other source

2 Idea is explained to cabinet

3 Cabinet approves idea

The Government and Opposition

In the House of Commons, MPs sit with other members of their political party. The party that holds the greatest number of seats in the House of Commons is known as the government. As you have seen, the leader of that party is the prime minister. All the MPs from the other parties are known as "Her Majesty's Loyal Opposition." Usually the leader of the second-largest party usually becomes the **Leader of the Opposition**.

The role of the Opposition is to ensure that the views of all Canadians are represented in Parliament, especially those who did not vote for the party that forms the government. It is the duty of Opposition MPs to criticize government policy with which they do not agree and to put forward their own ideas. Citizens can then know that they have alternatives if they become displeased with the party in power.

Four days a week, time is set aside for **question period**. At this time, Opposition members can raise issues and question government actions. The aim is to keep the government accountable for its actions. Because question period is lively, it often appears on television news. In this way, the Opposition can gather public attention and force the government to deal with issues it might prefer to ignore.

Leader of the Opposition: The leader of the second-largest party in the House of Commons.

question period: The time put aside for Opposition parties to raise issues and question the government.

The House of Commons. Members of the government sit facing the Opposition, so named because of this seating arrangement. By tradition, the House of Commons is decorated in green, and the distance between the government and Opposition benches is equal to two sword lengths. These traditions are based on old British customs.

House Leaders and Party Whips

Some MPs have additional roles in the House of Commons. House leaders help to develop strategies for other MPs from their party. For example, the house leader might suggest tactics for question period. House leaders also negotiate with other parties regarding timetables or procedures for issues to be debated.

Party whips work with house leaders, especially in deciding on tactics. For example, a whip might ensure that all members are present for a vote on a bill, so that it passes.

Occasionally, party whips discipline MPs who do not behave as expected by their party.

Every year, 40 high school students are selected from across the country to work as pages in the House of Commons. Pages serve primarily as messengers for members of Parliament.

The Senate

The Senate is referred to as the "upper house of Parliament." The Senate may propose a bill or amend bills passed by the House of Commons. It can also investigate issues that the House of Commons cannot or will not examine.

Senators are not elected. They are appointed by the governor general on the recommendation of the prime minister. Members of the Senate must be Canadian citizens, at least 30 years of age, and live in the province or territory they represent. In addition, they must own at least $4000 worth of property, and may serve until they are 75 years of age.

You will learn more about the role of the Senate in Chapter 5.

Did You Know?

Only Ontario refers to its provincial representatives as "MPP" (Member of Provincial Parliament). Most other provinces use the term "MLA" (Member of the Legislative Assembly).

The Legislative Branch at the Provincial Level

At the provincial level, the parliament is usually called the legislature or the legislative assembly. In Newfoundland, the provincial parliament is called the House of Assembly, and in Quebec it is the National Assembly. The legislatures of provinces and territories are modelled on the House of Commons. However, the provinces and territories do not have an "upper house" equivalent to the Senate. Once a bill is passed by a majority in the legislature, it goes directly to the lieutenant-governor for royal assent.

Thelma Chalifoux
Senator

Senator Thelma Chalifoux is the first Aboriginal woman to become a senator in Canada. She was born in Alberta, with roots in the Métis community that go back many generations. She was raised among relatives who worked for the rights of the Métis.

Chalifoux began her career as a field worker, first with the Métis Association of Alberta and then with a government agency called the Company of Young Canadians. She travelled through northern Alberta, helping Métis communities to improve their living conditions. She also helped community members work with their local governments and establish vocational centres and support groups. In recognition of her work, Chalifoux received a National Aboriginal Achievement Award.

When Chalifoux was appointed to the Senate, she discovered that her fellow senators and the general public knew very little about Aboriginal peoples. She has used her position in the Senate to educate Canadians about the different languages, cultures, and histories of Aboriginal Nations in Canada. She is a member of the Senate Standing Committee of Aboriginal Peoples.

Chalifoux also makes a point of speaking on behalf of the vibrant French communities of

northern Alberta — communities that are also largely unknown to the rest of the country.

"If you forget where you come from," says Chalifoux, "then you've lost sight of what you're supposed to be doing." Her position as senator gives her the power to be able to help more people. She feels that she is now in a situation to "make real and lasting changes."

What Is the Judicial Branch?

judicial branch: Branch of government with power to interpret the law, decide who has broken the law, and what penalties should apply.

The **judicial branch** is the part of government that deals with the law. In Canada, this branch is separate from the other two branches. This ensures that Parliament and its members are not above the law.

The judicial branch is made up of the courts and the judges. They determine if people charged with crimes are guilty or innocent and decide on punishments for those found guilty. They also interpret laws when disputes arise between individuals, groups, or even different levels of government.

The court system gives people the power to challenge actions or laws that they feel may threaten their rights. If, for example, the government brings forward an unfair law, any citizen has the right to take the issue through the court system.

There are two court systems in Canada: civil and criminal. The civil court system deals with the protection of private rights, such as disputes between individuals or groups of people. The criminal court system deals with offences against the public or against society.

Infosource 4–7 ▼ COURT STRUCTURE

This chart shows the typical court structure in Canada. There are some variations in titles and purposes among the provinces and territories.

APPEAL DIVISION

Supreme Court of Canada
(Handles some appeals from lower courts, including Provincial Supreme Court)

Provincial Supreme Court
(Handles some appeals from lower courts)

Court of Appeal
(General appeal court)

CRIMINAL DIVISION

Superior Court
(Major criminal cases)

Criminal Court
(Ordinary criminal cases)

CIVIL DIVISION

Civil Court
(Private disputes)

Small Claims Court
(Private disputes below $3000)

Family Court
(Custody, divorce, etc.)

Source: Foundations: Structure and Function of Government.

In both court systems, a citizen first brings an issue to a provincial court. If unsuccessful, the case can be taken to a higher provincial court for an appeal — that is, a request that the higher court reconsider the decision of the lower court. The Supreme Court of Canada is the court of final appeal. It hears appeals that have already been decided in the lower provincial courts.

The Supreme Court of Canada considers only cases of public interest or cases involving important points of law. The decision of the Supreme Court is final, since there can be no further appeals of its decisions. Because the members of the Supreme Court have the power to interpret the law, they are very powerful. They are appointed by Parliament, based on their history of service to the legal system and the people of Canada.

Very few Canadians are involved in court cases that make their way to the Supreme Court. Many more are involved with provincial courts.

Judges in the Supreme Court of Canada must not be involved in any political activities, cannot hold any other paid position, and must retire at age 75.

ACTIVITIES THE INQUIRING CITIZEN

BE Informed

1. Explain the general duties of **a)** the legislative branch, and **b)** the judicial branch of government.

2. Who is the MPP for your riding? Who is your federal MP? Prepare a biographical sketch of one of these representatives. Ensure you include the following information:
   - the name of your riding
   - how long the MP or MPP has represented your riding
   - his or her political party; his or her special responsibilities, if any
   - his or her job before becoming an MP or MPP
   - the best way to contact him or her
   - ways in which he or she keeps people informed about important issues

3. Imagine you were to interview Thelma Chalifoux. Write three to five questions you would ask her.

BE Purposeful

4. Why do you think bills must go through the steps shown in Infosource 4–6, before becoming law? How does the process benefit citizens?

5. Is it important, in a democratic society, to have a judicial branch that is separate from the other branches of government? Why or why not?

How Do We Select Our Representatives?

election: The process of voting to choose government representatives.

As you have seen, important decisions are made in Parliament — decisions that affect all Canadians. What gives our members of Parliament this power? The answer lies in our system of **elections**. When we vote for a candidate, we are giving him or her the power to make key decisions on our behalf. With our votes, we can seek to elect representatives who share our values and priorities. We can also refuse to vote for those representatives whose past performance has disappointed us.

Because our representatives are powerful, it is important to participate in elections. Nevertheless, many eligible citizens do not vote for a variety of reasons. Some withhold their votes to protest against government actions. Others believe that their vote will not influence election results, and therefore they do not bother to vote. Yet the difference of a few votes sometimes determines who is elected. When individuals do not vote, the votes of others become more influential. Citizens who do not exercise their right to vote are losing their chance to influence the decision-making process.

Responsible Government

What does this cartoon say about the importance of participating?

Once elected, our representatives — or members of Parliament — perform the daily business of governing our nation. They must follow

B.C.   by johnny hart

the rules for decision making as described earlier in this chapter. Elected representatives are responsible (accountable) for their actions to the people who elected them. For this reason, our form of government is called **responsible government**. All elected governments make decisions in the name of the people they represent.

Our MPs and MPPs hold the authority to use the power given to them by the people. It is important to remember that the powers of governments in Canada are given to them by citizens — and this power can be taken away at the next election. In this way, power rests *indirectly* with each individual citizen of Canada.

responsible government: A democratic system of government in which citizens vote for representatives. These representatives make decisions on behalf of the citizens.

Representation by Population

Elections provide a system for choosing the people who will represent us in many different situations. For instance, your student council may be selected according to a one-representative-per-class principle. This means that each class is allowed to elect one, and only one, member to the council. As shown in Infosource 4–8, the person in each class who gets the most votes wins.

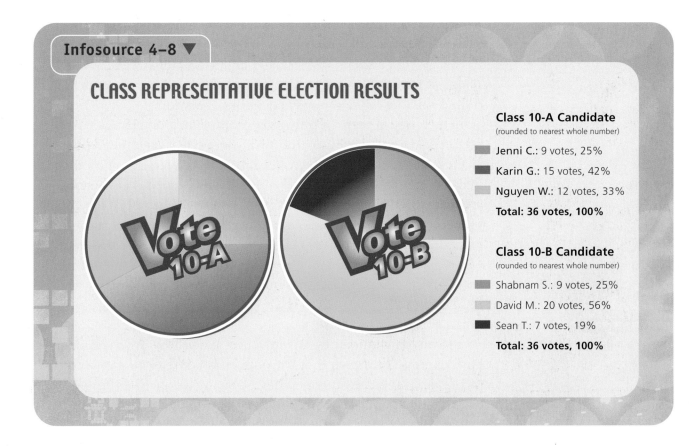

Infosource 4–8 ▼

CLASS REPRESENTATIVE ELECTION RESULTS

Class 10-A Candidate
(rounded to nearest whole number)

- Jenni C.: 9 votes, 25%
- Karin G.: 15 votes, 42%
- Nguyen W.: 12 votes, 33%

Total: 36 votes, 100%

Class 10-B Candidate
(rounded to nearest whole number)

- Shabnam S.: 9 votes, 25%
- David M.: 20 votes, 56%
- Sean T.: 7 votes, 19%

Total: 36 votes, 100%

representation by population: The principle that representation should be based proportionally on population.

Although federal and provincial elections in Canada are on a much larger scale, the underlying principle is similar to a student council election. This principle is called **representation by population**. This also means that the greater the number of people who live in a province or territory, the more members of Parliament that province or territory has in the federal government.

Ridings

riding or constituency: An area that has its own member of Parliament.

For the purposes of both federal and provincial representation and voting, each province is divided into **ridings**, also called **constituencies**. Ontario, for example, is divided into 103 ridings. The people who live within the boundaries of a riding are allowed to elect one representative to the provincial government. The candidate who receives the largest number of votes in each riding becomes its representative. In Ontario, these 103 elected members make up the government. This system is formally known as a "single-member plurality system":

- "Single member" means there is one representative per riding.

- "Plurality" means the winning candidate has received more votes than any other candidate, but not necessarily a majority.

Ideally, all ridings should have the same number of people, so that there is one elected representative for a set number of citizens. In this way, all citizens' votes would count equally. In reality, this is almost impossible to achieve. Instead, the system aims to have ridings that are approximately equal in population.

The physical size of a riding varies. Imagine, for example, a provincial riding in central Toronto where one representative is to be elected by 100 000 people (close to the actual average in Ontario). Because urban population is often very dense, especially where there are many high-rise buildings, a city riding might be only a few square kilometres. Compare this with a riding in the far north of the province that has a sparse population. In rural areas, the boundaries of a riding might need to be several hundred square kilometres to include 100 000 people. As a result, some of the constituencies in rural Ontario have less than the average population, while some urban constituencies have more.

As the population of Canada's cities has grown, urban residents have expressed concern that the population differences between urban and rural constituencies have become too great. Some people feel that city populations are under-represented, especially in provincial legislatures.

Did You Know?

The largest federal constituency in area is the entire territory of Nunavut, with 3 117 463 km². Even with this vast area, Nunavut has only 17 397 voters.

Infosource 4–9 ▼

Questioning Urban Under-representation

According to the 1997 census, at least 77.8 per cent of Canadians live inside what StatsCan calls CMAs, Census Metropolitan Areas. The rest of the world calls CMAs "cities." If you live in a city you are invariably under-represented in your provincial legislature.

The reason why is simple, and it applies across the country. The Supreme Court of Canada, in its wisdom, has decreed that both federal and provincial governments can draw electoral boundaries that favour rural areas. In a recent series of decisions, the court accepted the arguments made by the country mice that it is all right for sparsely populated parts of Canada to be over-represented by as much as 25 per cent. What that means in concrete terms is that it takes fewer farmers than urbanites to elect a provincial representative. Provincial governments draw the obvious conclusion: it's far more important to keep a rural voter happy than an urban one. Provincial administrations will never correct this problem, because they have no interest in changing the rules by which they won and maintain power.

Source: Calgary Herald

ACTIVITIES THE INQUIRING CITIZEN

BE Informed

1. What are the duties of an elected representative?

2. Re-examine Infosource 4–8.
   a) Who won in class 10-A? Was this person the choice of more than half the class?
   b) Who won in class 10-B? Was this person the choice of more than half the class?
   c) Who came second in class 10-B? How many votes did this person get? How does this result compare with that in class 10-A?
   d) Are these results democratic? Explain your position.

3. Explain the complaint voiced in Infosource 4–9. What arguments might rural voters make to justify their over-representation?

BE Purposeful

4. In Australia, it is compulsory for citizens to vote. Should voting be compulsory in Canada? Give three reasons to support your position.

BE Active

5. Prepare an information brochure for new Canadians on how we elect our representatives. Explain who can vote, responsible government, representation by population, and ridings.

How Well Do Our Representatives Reflect Our Population?

As well as the issue of rural/urban balance, there are other questions on whether our population is fairly represented. Historically, most government representatives have been middle-aged men of British or French background. Often these men had careers in law or business. Obviously, they only reflected a small part of Canadian society.

Can representatives make decisions in our best interests if they do not share our background and experiences? If not, there are several groups of Canadian citizens who do not have enough of a voice in federal and provincial government. Considering they make up half the population, women are still under-represented, both as candidates and as elected members. If the 103 seats in the Ontario legislature were to be filled so the population was accurately reflected, 50 per cent of the seats would be filled by women, 50 per cent by men. According to the following Infosources, is the representation of women in politics getting any better?

Up to the year 2000, Canada had only one woman prime minister, Kim Campbell *(left)*. Sheila Copps *(right)* had been Canada's only woman deputy prime minister. Both held these offices for only a short period of time.

An Insider's View on Female Representatives

During the life of Canada's Parliament, we have elected 81 women and 3485 men. Obviously there's something wrong with a system that disproportionately sends one gender to Parliament in such great numbers.

Deputy Prime Minister Sheila Copps, speaking to the Royal Commission on Electoral Reform on Women's Issues [1993]

Status of Female Candidates in the Federal Election, 1997

At the federal general election in 1997, there were 1672 candidates.... There were 408 women, making up 24.4 per cent of the candidates, as compared to 22.1 per cent in 1993. The New Democratic Party had the highest proportion of female candidates: 35.5 per cent. The Bloc Québécois had 21.3 per cent; the Liberals 20.8 per cent; Progressive Conservatives 18.0 per cent; and the Reform Party 9.0 per cent.

Federal Political Representation, 2000

HOUSE OF COMMONS

Political Party	Number of Women	Number of Men
Liberal	36	121
Bloc Québécois	11	33
Canadian Alliance	3	54
New Democrats	7	13
Progressive Conservative	3	15
Independent	0	4
TOTAL*	60	240

*Plus 1 vacant seat

SENATE

	Number of Women	Number of Men
Liberal	20	35
Progressive Conservative	11	29
Independent	1	4
TOTAL*	32	68

*Plus 5 vacant seats

Source: Adapted from http://www.parl.gc.ca/36/refmat/library/ASP/StandingsWomen.asp?Language=E&Source=S

Racial and cultural minority groups are also under-represented. As Canada becomes more multicultural, our need for more mixed representation increases. By the late 1990s, only 3 per cent of representatives in the federal government were from cultural minorities, although cultural minorities made up more than 6 per cent of the population. Only three members of Parliament were Aboriginal.

Some of the representatives who reflect Canada's diverse population. **Left to right:** Ujjal Dosanjh; David Tsubouchi; Ethel Blondin-Andrew.

ANALYZING THE ISSUE

BE Informed

1. In your own words, identify the issue raised in this section.

2. What evidence is provided to suggest that elected representatives do not reflect our population?

BE Purposeful

3. What characteristics or experience, other than cultural background, might make someone able to represent a wide variety of citizens?

4. How important do you think it is for representatives to reflect the population? Give three reasons to support your view.

BE Active

5. In small groups, brainstorm ideas that might help to make the people we elect more representative of our communities. Choose the best three ideas and prepare a brief to be presented to a government task force on the issue.

What Are Political Parties?

Most candidates who run in elections for our federal or provincial governments belong to a political party. A **political party** is a group of people who share an ideology. They work to elect candidates with similar beliefs.

Because parties often take different views on various issues, voters will support the party with whose views they agree. Only a small percentage of Canadian voters actually belong to a political party. However, many do consistently support the candidates of one party.

Those who want to belong to a party join the party's riding association. Once they become members, they can nominate candidates for their party and help to decide on the **party platform**, the statement of where the party stands on major political issues. If the party can attract enough voters, its candidates will be elected. If enough candidates from the party are elected, it will form the next government. The party will then be able to create laws that reflect its views.

political party: An organization of people with similar views on public issues who work to elect their candidates.

party platform: The proposals put forward by a political party during an election campaign.

Infosource 4–13 ▼   POLITICAL SPECTRUM

People who study politics sometimes use a political "spectrum" to explain the range of beliefs and views on a civic issue. In this political spectrum, beliefs and views are categorized "left-wing," "centre," or "right-wing." Often political parties are linked with these categories.

LEFT-WING	CENTRE	RIGHT-WING
Support change in order to improve the welfare of all citizens.	Tradition is important, but change must be supported if most people want it.	Tradition is important; change should be treated with caution.
Governments should play a larger role in people's lives, especially in providing social services.	Governments should play a role only in that it improves the lives of citizens.	Governments should play a small role. Private businesses should ensure needs of citizens are met.
Law and order are important to protect the rights of all citizens fairly and equally.	Law and order are important to encourage and protect rights of individuals.	Emphasizes law and order to protect society and its traditions.

Canada's Major Political Parties

Some of Canada's political parties at the federal level are shown in Infosource 4–14. The largest of these are the Bloc Québécois, the Liberal Party, the New Democratic Party, the Progressive Conservative Party, and the Canadian Reform Conservative Alliance, formerly the Reform Party. Since Confederation in 1867, only the Conservatives and the Liberals have formed a government at the federal level.

Some of the parties shown, such as the Bloc Québécois, exist only at the federal level. There are also some parties at the provincial level that do not operate at the federal level. Some of Canada's political parties are new, and there are some parties that were once active at either the federal or provincial level, but no longer exist. Some of the parties, such as the Green Party and the Communist Party, have never had success in elections in Canada, but do have continuing support.

Infosource 4–14 ▼

REGISTERED FEDERAL POLITICAL PARTIES

Bloc Québécois
Canadian Action Party
Canadian Reform Conservative Alliance
Christian Heritage Party
Communist Party of Canada
The Green Party of Canada

Liberal Party of Canada
Marxist-Leninist Party of Canada
Natural Law Party of Canada
New Democratic Party
Progressive Conservative Party of Canada

Canada's New Democrats

BLOC QUÉBÉCOIS

Liberal

PC
Progressive Conservative Party of Canada
Parti progressiste-conservateur du Canada

CANADIAN ALLIANCE CANADIENNE

Official Party Status

All political parties must register their name, address, and other details with the chief electoral officer of Canada. If they satisfy certain requirements, they can receive official party status, which has certain benefits (see Infosource 4–15).

Party Candidates and Independents

Most candidates who run in an election belong to a political party. Parties give their candidates a great deal of help, including print, radio, and television advertising. A candidate who does not belong to a party may run as an **independent**. However, most independents do not have enough money or workers to mount an effective campaign and rarely get much media attention. For these reasons, it is difficult for an independent candidate to win.

Although elected representatives are responsible to their ridings, they also need to be loyal to their parties. The party expects its elected members to support its goals and policies. When the wishes of the voters in the riding differ from those of the party, the representative may be caught in the middle.

Infosource 4–15 ▼

Official Party Status

Requirements

- The party must officially nominate candidates in 50 ridings, and must have 12 elected MPs.
- The party must have submitted a registration application at least 60 days before the election.

Benefits

- The party name appears beside the candidate's name on ballots.
- The party has access to paid and free broadcasting.
- Party members can ask questions daily in Parliament.

independent: A candidate or elected member who does not belong to a political party.

ACTIVITIES   THE INQUIRING CITIZEN

BE Informed

1. What is the role of political parties in Canada?

2. Which parties play a role in politics in your province? How would you place each of these parties on a political spectrum?

BE Active

3. **a)** Investigate the Web site of any registered political party in Canada.

b) Prepare a political poster that gives a brief outline of the party's history, the party's leader, its strength in your province, three important beliefs held by the party, and three important policies on which it is working. Include the party logo and details about how to find additional information on the party.

What Happens During an Election Campaign?

Did You Know?

A **by-election** is an election held for a vacant seat or a group of vacant seats, rather than all seats in a general election. By-elections occur when an elected representative retires, dies, or chooses to leave a seat before a general election.

Political parties are always working to increase their public support and prepare for the next election campaign. But when does an election campaign actually begin? A general election at the federal level formally begins when the prime minister calls on the governor general to "dissolve Parliament." This means ending the Parliament that is currently underway. A federal election must be held at least every five years, but can be held sooner if the prime minister believes it is necessary — or if the government party has lost an important vote, such as a vote on its proposed budget.

All federal elections are carried out under the authority of the chief electoral officer. Individual ridings are organized by returning

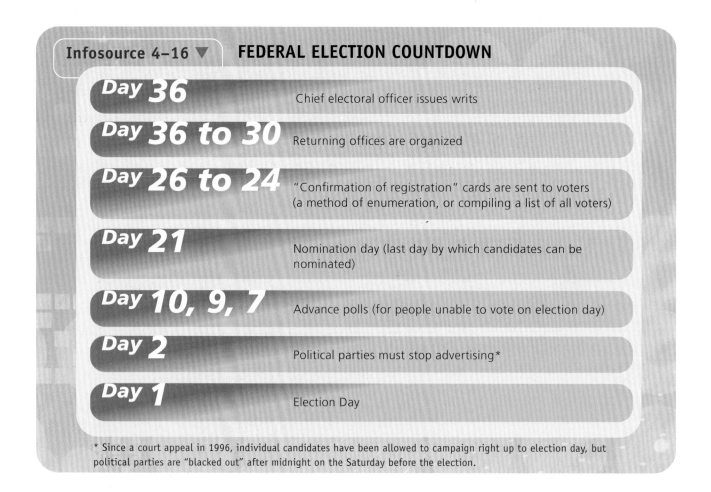

Infosource 4–16 ▼ **FEDERAL ELECTION COUNTDOWN**

Day 36 — Chief electoral officer issues writs

Day 36 to 30 — Returning offices are organized

Day 26 to 24 — "Confirmation of registration" cards are sent to voters (a method of enumeration, or compiling a list of all voters)

Day 21 — Nomination day (last day by which candidates can be nominated)

Day 10, 9, 7 — Advance polls (for people unable to vote on election day)

Day 2 — Political parties must stop advertising*

Day 1 — Election Day

* Since a court appeal in 1996, individual candidates have been allowed to campaign right up to election day, but political parties are "blacked out" after midnight on the Saturday before the election.

officers. As soon as the chief electoral officer is notified that Parliament is dissolved, he or she prepares writs of election, the official documents to set the election in motion. This is the beginning of intense activity by Elections Canada employees, political parties and their candidates, advisors and volunteers, and the media.

Provincial election campaigns are very similar to federal ones. The provincial premier calls on the lieutenant-governor to dissolve the provincial legislature. The electoral officer for the province then issues the writs. In Ontario, the campaign lasts 28 days.

Politicians on the campaign trail *(clockwise from top left)*: greeting campaign workers; speaking on radio shows; talking with constituents; dealing with the media.

Did You Know?

Until April 1997, voters were enumerated (placed on the voting list) by door-to-door surveys. Now lists of voters are generated using the National Register of Electors, an electronic database that is updated regularly.

Competing for Voter Support

Once an official election date is announced, the competition for voter support begins. Candidates' signs spring up on lawns and in shop windows overnight. Citizens are deluged with campaign literature, notices of rallies and town hall meetings, and newspaper and television coverage. Candidates inform potential voters of their qualifications and beliefs. Party platforms are explained and plans presented. Through advertising and debates, the policies of other parties are criticized.

Infosource 4–17 ▼ **NEGATIVE ADVERTISING**

A panel of five advertising executives was asked to evaluate the television ads of the three major parties during a recent election in Ontario....

The panel took the Liberals to task for the "Mean Mike" spot, which began with a clip of the Conservative premier saying "There's going to be one mean, mad Mike Harris," followed by footage of riot police cracking down on striking civil servants and stretchers in overcrowded emergency ward hallways. The problem is that Harris was referring to another issue entirely when he said the quoted words, so it is taken out of context.

The Conservatives were also criticized for misrepresenting other parties.

Source: Adapted from Toronto Star

This billboard advertisement was placed by a group opposed to Ontario's NDP government (1991–1995). The premier at that time was Bob Rae, shown on the right-hand side. What do you think of this kind of advertising? Is it effective? Is it fair?

KILLS BUGS   KILLS MICE   KILLS JOBS

ONTARIANS FOR RESPONSIBLE GOVERNMENT (416) 869-3838

The media play a vital role in election campaigns. They inform voters of debates, rallies, town hall meetings, party statements, social events, and parades held by candidates and the parties. They provide free air time for all registered parties to present their party platform and candidates. And, of course, they cover all appearances by the leaders and other newsworthy candidates of the major parties. You will read more about media involvement in Canadian politics in Chapter 5.

In recent years, there has been a concern that media campaigns have become nastier. Negative advertising, which attacks the opposing candidate or party, has become more common. Many people think negative advertising cheapens our politicians and causes a loss of respect for the winners, who must then govern us. Others argue that despite some of the drawbacks of nasty campaigns, they get citizens involved in the election by causing strongly positive or negative reactions. Finally, it is unclear whether negative advertising actually works.

ACTIVITIES   THE INQUIRING CITIZEN

BE Informed

1. **a)** Examine the photographs on page 131. What strategies is each of these politicians using to gain support?
   b) What other strategies do politicians and political parties use to gain support?

BE Purposeful

2. What would you want to know about candidates in an election before you voted?
   a) Take an informal poll of your classmates to find out what information most of them would want to know about political candidates.
   b) Now poll people who voted in the last election to find out what they think people should know about candidates.

c) Make a checklist that you could use as a guide when deciding which candidate to choose in an election.

BE Active

3. Working in a small group, review the information presented so far in this chapter. Imagine that your group is going to create a political party. What beliefs would be central to your party? What would be your goals for Ontario or for Canada? Prepare a political advertisement for an upcoming election that gives your party's name, logo, and platform, including key ideological beliefs and three policy proposals. Present your advertisement to the class, and see what support you receive.

Detecting Bias

A **bias** is a one-sided view about something, someone, or an issue. It is often a prejudice or preconceived opinion — an opinion formed without evidence or proper reason. We all have biases that are based on our own experiences or preferences. It is important, however, to recognize someone else's bias, especially when the bias appears in the media or other form of information.

Follow these steps to help in detecting bias.

■ Identify the source of information. Is this source known to have a particular point of view about the issue being discussed?

■ Look for clues to bias:
   Is the language emotional?
   Is there any exaggeration?
   Are there any obvious gaps in factual information?
   Is only one side of the issue presented?

■ Identify specific examples of bias.

Try to read several different sources on the same topic. In this way you will get a range of views that will help you form your own opinion about the issue.

Putting It Into Practice

1. Using the steps above, review the poster on page 132 for bias. Compare responses with a partner.

2. As a class, discuss what challenges you encountered in trying to detect bias in the infosource.

3. Why do you think it is important for citizens to be able to detect bias in the media? Brainstorm ways in which citizens can protect themselves from media bias.

How Can We Participate?

There are a number of ways we can participate in political parties and elections. As you have seen, people who join political parties can nominate candidates and they can help to define the party's views on political issues. They can also participate in choosing the party's leaders, and many help to raise funds for the party.

At election time, there are many additional ways to participate, as shown in Infosource 4–18.

Infosource 4–18 ▼

Volunteer Jobs in an Election Campaign

- **Foot canvasser:** Going door to door to identify potential voters and to give information
- **Phone canvasser:** Phoning individuals to identify potential support and give information
- **Sign team:** Delivering and installing signs for lawns, storefronts, or apartment buildings to supporters
- **Communication team:** Helping to design and produce literature for the campaign
- **Media relations:** Dealing with the media and working on press releases
- **Research:** Doing research for the candidate's speeches or on local issues
- **Fundraising:** Approaching individuals or groups for money to run the campaign
- **Election-day inside scrutineer:** Working in a poll on election day to keep track of who has voted and to count ballots at the end of the day
- **Election-day outside scrutineer:** Taking lists of supporters in a poll and making sure they vote by the end of the day

Source: Adapted from OSSTF/FEESO

Volunteers for the Parti Québécois make last-minute phone calls to remind supporters to vote in their provincial election.

Young people can become involved in party work, even before they reach voting age. Some parties have youth wings, specifically to attract young members like you. There are political youth groups at most universities and even at some high schools. The parties hope to attract young supporters to ensure a more secure future for the party. There are also benefits for those who participate.

Infosource 4–19 ▼

Young Citizen's Field Work Assignment, June 1999

June 3 was an important day for 7 million Ontarians. Their quality of life for the next five years was to be decided that day. Which political party would it be? To learn and experience what an election was all about, I volunteered to help out at the Liberals' campaign office. I had read the literature that was dropped at our house and made my decision on that basis.

I did a lot of work from sorting folders to telephone canvassing. The many hours of volunteering taught me many things, especially because it gave me an insight as to how voters decide on their choices. Some voters wanted to know more about the candidates to help them make their choice. On the other hand, many voters did not know who the candidates were, but were willing to support a particular party.

By Han Na Kim, grade 10 student

In Chapter 2, you looked at the issue of whether or not Canadians under 18 should be eligible to vote. In what other ways can young people contribute to the election process?

YOUTH GROUPS PARTICIPATE AT PARTY CONVENTIONS

Jeff Wagner of the Progressive Conservative Youth Federation is a grade 12 student. He feels that youth groups play a key role in improving the capabilities of tomorrow's politicians. "Youth leaders are getting the education to become better leaders in the community," he says. "If you want to play hockey, you join the hockey team." But youth joining in the political process can be helpful, regardless of what their career plans are, Wagner maintains. "We need an educated and concerned public," he says.

Université de Moncton student Bruno Roy, recently retired head of the Young Liberals of Canada, also finds that conventions are the most productive forum for putting suggestions to the party. In the biennial convention of the Liberal party... the Young Liberals put forward a number of new initiatives. Resolutions presented were first discussed in local groups, which exist in nearly every campus in the country.

"The Young Liberals are trying to be the social conscience of the party and the progressive element," says Roy.... While not binding to the party, a vote often leads to modification of its platform. "If you're not radical when you're young," he says, quoting the prime minister, "you're going to get old soon."

Source: Adapted from TG Magazine/The Students Commission

ACTIVITIES — THE INQUIRING CITIZEN

BE Informed

1. How did Han Na Kim choose which party to work for in the election? What other criteria might she have used to make her decision?

2. Review Infosource 4–20.
   a) According to Jeff Wagner and Bruno Roy, what are the advantages of political party youth groups?
   b) What other reasons might people have for joining a political youth group?

BE Purposeful

3. **a)** Imagine that you are joining a political party in your community. What jobs could you do to help the local association or candidate during elections? What could you do to help between elections?
   b) Do you think responsible citizens have a duty to get involved in a political party? Why or why not?

4. If you decided to run as a candidate in an election, would you join a political party first? Why or why not? If you would, which party would you join? Give reasons for your choice.

Voters choose only one candidate by marking an "X" in the circle next to the candidate's name.

Winning the Election

On election night, after everyone has voted, government officials count the ballots. Every election in Canada has officials to watch over the process and to ensure it is completed according to the rules and regulations. They make sure:

- The election date is advertised.
- Candidates fill out the proper forms.
- The list of voters is accurate.
- Polling stations (where votes are cast) are advertised, properly staffed, and ready.
- Ballots are printed with accurate information.
- Votes are counted accurately and fairly.
- Winners are declared quickly and correctly.

When the ballots are counted, the method used to decide the winner in each constituency is known as **first past the post (FPTP)**. The candidate who wins the most votes is elected.

Consider how this system influenced the outcome of the election shown in Infosource 4–21. In the Ontario riding of Algoma-Manitoulin, in the provincial election of 1999, more people voted against Mike Brown than voted for him. However, he had more votes than any other single candidate, and by the system we use in Canada, he won the election.

The party that wins the election is also the one that is the first past the post. In other words, the party that wins the most ridings has the most seats in Parliament, and usually forms the government. This party rarely wins 50 per cent or more of the vote. For example, a party

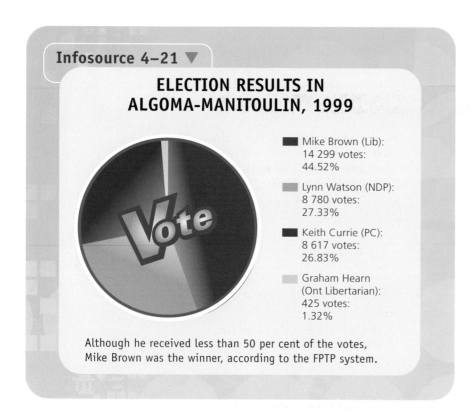

Infosource 4–21 ▼

ELECTION RESULTS IN ALGOMA-MANITOULIN, 1999

- Mike Brown (Lib): 14 299 votes: 44.52%
- Lynn Watson (NDP): 8 780 votes: 27.33%
- Keith Currie (PC): 8 617 votes: 26.83%
- Graham Hearn (Ont Libertarian): 425 votes: 1.32%

Although he received less than 50 per cent of the votes, Mike Brown was the winner, according to the FPTP system.

that came second in every single riding might receive a very large number of votes overall, but would have no seats at all. This extreme outcome has never actually happened in Canadian politics, but it could.

ONTARIO'S PROVINCIAL ELECTION, 1999

Registered political parties	Candidates elected	Valid ballots cast	% of total valid ballots
Communist Party	-	814	-
Ontario Provincial Confederation of Regions Party	-	282	-
Family Coalition Party	-	24 216	0.6
Freedom Party	-	4 806	0.1
Green Party	-	30 749	0.7
Liberal Party	35	1 751 472	39.9
Libertarian Party	-	2 337	0.1
Natural Law Party	-	19 491	0.4
New Democratic Party	9	551 009	12.6
Progressive Conservative Party	59	1 978 059	45.1
Reform Party	-	174	-

ACTIVITIES   THE INQUIRING CITIZEN

BE Informed

1. Examine Infosource 4–22 to determine whether each of the following statements can be supported by the statistics provided. Explain your answer. Rewrite each false statement to make it true.

   a) The percentage of total seats a party wins will match the percentage of the popular vote (the total number of votes cast by voters) that it receives.

   b) In our electoral system, the seats are fairly shared based on the support for each party in the province.

   c) A party can win a majority of the seats in the legislature (50% + 1) without gaining a majority of all the votes.

BE Purposeful

2. Explain how the rules and regulations for fair elections protect democratic practices. What other rules might make elections fairer or more democratic?

Making a Presentation

Anyone involved in politics knows the importance of making a presentation — in public settings, such as campaign speeches, or information situations, such as door-to-door canvassing. Many people are nervous about speaking in front of a group. The key to overcoming a fear of public speaking is to be well prepared. Here are some helpful hints.

- Research your topic thoroughly.

- Develop a detailed outline of what you want to say.

- Determine the reason for your speech. Do you want to inform, persuade, or entertain the audience?

- Know your audience. Are you speaking to a large or small group? What kind of speech will appeal to these people? Can you involve them in any way?

- Check how much time you have for your presentation. Make sure you have enough, but not too much, to say.

- Use visual aids. Consider charts, pictures, maps, etc. Make sure the equipment you need is available.

Making a presentation also requires practice. Get a friend or family member to listen to you do a practice run of your presentation, or use a tape recorder. The more you practise, the more confident you will become.

Putting It Into Practice

1. Choose a current issue related to provincial or federal government. Prepare a presentation on this issue, using the steps above. Your presentation might take the form of a political speech, newscast, or presentation to a committee meeting.

2. Take turns making your presentations. Work in groups to give each other constructive advice on how the presentations could be improved.

3. As a class, discuss the challenges you faced in making your presentations. Why do you think it is important for citizens to be able to make effective presentations?

Does Canada Need to Reform Its Electoral System?

Some Canadians feel that our electoral system is not fair, and that it should be reformed. Consider some of the following views.

Infosource 4–23 ▼

FIRST PAST THE POST JUST DOESN'T CUT IT

The present system is broken. First past the post is so named because a candidate has only to win more votes than his nearest competitor to take the riding, not an absolute majority of the votes cast. The most direct consequence is to exaggerate the majority enjoyed by the winning party: with less than half the popular vote, governments have been formed with nearly all of the seats…. It produces results that are increasingly at odds with voters' desires.

Source: Adapted from Toronto Star

Infosource 4–24 ▼

FPTP'S SINGULAR VIRTUE IS STABILITY

FPTP's singular virtue is stability. Because the [FPTP] system produces more majority governments than minority ones, governments can usually get done what they wish to accomplish. FPTP leads to that old quip about parliamentary democracy being an "elected dictatorship."… Some smaller parties, such as the New Democrats and Reformers, have called for adopting forms of proportional representation. The big parties — the ones that usually win elections — won't hear of it.

Source: Adapted from Globe and Mail

As you can see, the first past the post system has its critics. The main argument against it is that the party forming the government doesn't necessarily represent the majority of the people — and usually does not. Our present method results in parliaments that may not accurately represent what the voters want. What does this say about how we are represented? Is there a better system? Here are some options to consider.

Proportional Representation System

The system of proportional representation (PR) is used in several other democracies — for example, Italy, Sweden, and Israel. In this system, voters do not elect individuals for their particular area. Instead they vote for a party, both nationally and regionally. Whatever percentage of the overall vote a party receives in the election is the percentage of seats it will be allotted in government. The PR system allows different groups to share power.

Most PR systems operate on a "list" basis. Each party puts forward a list of its candidates. The number of seats a party wins in the legislature is based on the number of votes it receives. In a 100-seat legislature, for example, a party that receives 38 per cent of the popular vote will elect candidates 1 to 38 on its list.

This system, however, is not without its problems. One objection is that voters in a PR system do not have local representatives. Another problem is that, since most elections do not give one party a majority, governments must be formed by coalitions between parties. In some countries, these coalitions cannot be maintained for very long. This increases the number of elections and weakens the stability of governments.

This ballot is from Holland, where PR is used. The ballot has been greatly reduced in size and only a portion is shown here. What disadvantages do you see with this ballot?

STEMBILJET voor de verkiezing van de leden van de Tweede K:

KANDIDATENLIJSTEN

1 Christen Democratisch Appèl (CDA)	1 Christen Democratisch Appèl (CDA) (vervolg)	2 Partij van de Arbeid (P.v.d.A.)	2 Partij van de Arbeid (P.v.d.A.) (vervolg)	3 V.V.D.	4 Democraten 66 (D66)	5 GROENLINKS	6 Staatkundig Gereformeerde Partij (gecombineerd met de lijsten 7 en 8)	7 Gereformeerd Politiek Verbond (GPV) (gecombineerd met de lijsten 6 en 8)	8 RPF (gecombineerd met de lijsten 6 en 7)	9 Centrum-democraten (CD)	10 De Nieuwe Partij	11 PSP'92	
Brinkman, L.C. Leiden		Kok, W. (Wim) Amsterdam		Bolkestein, F. (Frits) Amsterdam	van Mierlo, H.A.F.M.O. (Hans) Amsterdam	Brouwer (v), L. (Ina) Amsterdam	van der Vlies, Ir. B.J. Maartensdijk	Schutte, G.J. Zeist	van Dijke, L.C. (Leen) Middelburg	Janmaat, drs. J.G.H. 's-Gravenhage	Blase, A.B. (Bert) Sneek	Robroek, J.C.H. (Jos) Sneek	Mari J.G.
van Rooy (v), Y.C.M.T. 's-Gravenhage		Wallage, J. (Jacques) Haarlem		Terpstra (v), E.G. (Erica) Den Haag	Wolffens-perger, G.J. (Gerrit Jan) Amsterdam	Rabbae (m), M. (Mohamed) Maarssen	van den Berg, mr. dr. J.T. Nunspeet	van Middelkoop, E. Berkel en Rodenrijs	Schuurman (v), W.D. 's-Gravenhage	Schuurman (v), W.B. 's-Gravenhage	Edelenbosch, C. (Cor) Enkhuizen	Popp (Rem	
Hirsch Ballin, E.M.H. Tilburg		Wöltgens, M.A.M. (Thijs) Kerkrade		Dijkstal, Hans F. Wassenaar	Rosenmöller (m), P. (Paul) Rotterdam	van Heukelom, G.R.J. Nieuwerkerk	van Haeften, M.P.H. Den Haag	Zonneveld, C. Schiedam	Rouvoet, mr. A. (André) Nunspeet	van Brink, M.J. (Michel) Enschede	van ... C.J.I		
Deetman, W.J. Gouda		Adelmund, K.Y.I.J. (Karin) Amsterdam		Jorritsma geb. Lebbink, A. (Annemarie) Bolsward	Kohnstamm, J. (Jacob) Amsterdam	Sipkes geb. van Zijl (v), L. (Leoni) Apeldoorn	Noordergraaf, G.J. Hasselt	Elsthout, W. Haarlem	Stellingwerf, D.J. (Dick) Ede	Radhakishun, A.S.S. (Anand) Haarlem	Viss (Yvo		
Heerma, E. Amsterdam		Pronk, J.P. (Jan) 's-Gravenhage		Linschoten, R.L.O. (Robin) Dronten	Tommel, D.K.J. (Dick) Soest	Vos (v), M.B. (Marijke) Amsterdam	Wilcke geb. van der Linden (v), M. Hoevelaken	Giesen, drs. M.T. Zoetermeer	Kuiper, dr. R. (Roel) Eck en Wiel	van der Werf, D. (Daphne) Haarlem	van H.		
Soutendijk geb. van Appeldoorn, M.H.J. Nuenen		Kosto, A. (Aad) Grootschermer		Dees, D.J.D. Breda	Groenman, M.S. (Louise) Maarssen	Oedayraj Singh Varma (v), T. (Tara) Amsterdam	Holdijk, mr. G. Apeldoorn	de Keijne, J. Rotterdam	Hoek geb. van Kooten, drs. A.B.F. (Alie) Veenendaal	Davidse, C.J. (Cees) Apeldoorn	Koning, C.J. (Kees) Eindhoven	Bere M.J.	
Wolters, F.L.A.J. Venlo-Blerick		Alders, J.G.M. (Hans) Nijmegen		Franssen, J. Nederhorst den Berg	Nuis, A. (Aad) Maarssen	van Ree, drs. P.H.D. Lunteren	Crossen, S.J.C. Zwolle	Koning, ing. M. Dordrecht	Snijders, R. Zoetermeer	Dobson, W.R.E.J. (Bill) Middelburg	Kannegieter, P.A.A.B. (Paula) Assendelft	Sch (Mar	
de Hoop Scheffer, J.G. 's-Gravenhage		ter Beek, A.L. (Relus) Coevorden		de Korte, R.W. (Rudolf) Wassenaar	Scheltema geb. de Nie, O. (Olga) Haren	van Ojik (m), A. (Bram) Amsterdam	Blokland, J. Capelle aan den IJssel	ten Hove, drs. J.H. Katwijk	Voogt, mr. drs. S.O. Rotterdam	Repetur, M.E. (Lou)	van Liefland, R.M. (Renée) Heiloo (O)	Sch	
Lansink, A.J.W.J. Nijmegen		van der Ploeg, F. (Rick) Amsterdam		Weisglas, Frans W. Rotterdam	Schimmel, A.J. (Arthie) Amsterdam	van Gent (v), W. (Ineke) Groningen	Haak geb. Griffioen (v), M. Soest	Rietkerk, drs. W.G. Utrecht	Poppe, A.A.J. Vlissingen	Schijns, A.H. Haarlem	Stinis, Y.H. (Yvonne) Aarle-Rixtel	Jona (Pau	
Doelman geb. Pel, A. Hoogezand		Netelenbos geb. Koomen, T. (Tineke) Hoofddorp		van der Stoel (v), Anne Lize E.C.	Jorritsma geb. van Oosten, J.A. (Joke) Utrecht	Meijer (m), H. (Herman) Rotterdam	Alssema, J.D. Aduard	van Dam, mr. R. Barneveld	Datema, L.E. Haarlem	Berndsen, H.A.M. (Herma)	Bouma, W.R. (Wolf) Westervoort	Osk (Ber	
Bukman, P. Voorschoten		Melkert, A.P.W. (Ad) Almere		Korthals, A.H. (Johan) Uden	Lambrechts, E.D.C.M. (Ursie) Uden	Boonzaaijer, drs. G. Bilthoven	Haasdijk, Th. Hoogland	Frinsel, J.J. Montfoort	Verheij, C.G. Ridderkerk	Groeneweg, J. Rotterdam	Karman, E.A. (Erik) Heerhugowaard	van J.N.	
van der Linden, P.R.H.M. Nuth		Remkes, J.W. (Johan)		Ybema, G. (Gerrit) Leeuwarden	Pieters, W. Genemuiden	Groen, L.C. Bunschoten-Spakenburg	de Graaf, A. Ede	Pellegrom, B. Delft	van den Elst, R.E. (Rob) Eerrum	Wiebenga, H. (Hans) Bloemendaal	de Vries, F. (Fries) Amsterdam	Verg Mud Fen	
Boers geb. Wijnberg, M.H.A. Tilburg		Vermeend, W.A.F.G. (Willem) Leiden		Kamp (v), M.M.H. (Margreet) Vianen	Versnel geb. Schmitz, M.M. (Margreet)	den Uil, drs. P.C. Hendrik Ido Ambacht	de Vries, J.P. Amersfoort	de Boer, A. Zwolle	van der Spek, G.J.A.	Wissink, A.A. (Albert) Doetinchem	Heltmeijer, G. (Dies) Baarn	Corr T.S.	
van der Burg, V.A.M. Zeist		Oudkerk, R.H. (Rob) Amsterdam		van Hoof, H.A.L. (Henk) Alkmaar	Willems (m), W.J. (Wilbert) Tilburg	Scholten, L.M.P. Capelle a/d IJssel	van der Kolk (v), A.E.H. Harderwijk	Blokhuis, drs. P. Lunschoten	de Regt, M.H. Zeist	Nieland, R.J.L. (Robert-Jan) Amsterdam	Boon, H.J. (Henk)	van Horr Jos	
Beinema, M. Middelburg		Noorman geb. den Uyl, S.E.A. (Saskia) Heemstede		te Veldhuis, A.J. (Jan) Middelburg	Dittrich, B.O. (Boris) Amsterdam	de Visser (m), M.J. (Piet) Rotterdam	Stelpstra, T. Oudkarspel	Jochemsen, dr. ir. H. Bennekom	Gilles, J.A. Haarlem	van der Schoor, D.A. (Dieneke) Mijnsheerenland	Kiers, A.H. (Arnaud) Sneek	de Si	
van der Hoeven (v), M.J.A. Maastricht		Vreeman, R.L. (Ruud) Heemstede		van Erp, A.A.M.E. (Broos) Best	ter Veer, P.K. (Pieter) Wolterum	Lucas (v), M.J.J. (Marjan) Nijmegen	Lagendijk, J. Assen	Leering, Meindert Huizen	Noelen, F.J.M. Lelystad	Sipkema, J.N. Apeldoorn	Arts, J.C.C.B. (John) Amsterdam	de Ri Horr	
Gabor, J.D. Haaksbergen		van Zijl, J.P.C.M. (Jan) Voorburg		Blauw, Piet M. Veendam	Fermina, H.G. (Hubert) Dordrecht	Molier (v), J.E. (Jeannine) Den Haag	Bogerd, M. Urk	Hordijk, L. Hoogland	van Sitteren, W. Amsterdam	Rietveld, C.S. Hoorn	Lagerweij, A.B. (Alfred) Voorschoten	Macrander, W.J.A. (Wim) Amsterdam	Rue (Bo
Reitsma, J. Emmeloord		van Nieuwen-hoven, Jeltje Amsterdam		Voûte geb. Droste, W.C.G. (Hella) Aerdenhout	van 't Riet, N.G. (Nicky) Utrecht	Bisschop, dr. R. Veenendaal	de Boer, R. Kampen	Geersing, J. Schuinesloot	van de Kooi, J.C. Zwijndrecht	Hulst, H.C. (Hans) Harkstede	de Jong, T. (Toon) Nijmegen	Ser (Wie	
Mateman, W.A. Aalten		Duivesteijn, A.Th. (Adri) 's-Gravenhage		Kamp, H.G.J. (Henk) Borculo	Diepeveen (m), K. (Kees) Amsterdam	Budding, D.J. Elspeet	van de Groep, M. Bunschoten-Spakenburg	Dijkstra, P. Drachten	van der Kooi, J.C.	Rietel, G.F. Rotterdam	Kon, A.J. (Aris) Arnhem	J.R.	
van Ardenne		Buurmeijer, J.F. (Flip) Holten		van Rey, J.F.B. (Jos) Roermond	Augusteijn geb. Esser, M.J. (Marijke) Emmen	Hofmeijer (v), H.G.A. (Herma) Utrecht	Dankers, J. Waddinxveen	de Boer, P. Kampen	Warris, J. Stadskanaal	Stoops, D.J. 's-Gravenhage	Linssen, B.L.C. (Benno) Groot	Harr G.W.	
		van Traa, Maarten		de Koning,	de Graaf, Th. (Thom) Leiden	Suudi (m), R.V. (Radi) Amsterdam	van Heteren, A. Werkendam	van de Groep, M.	Pot, mr. J. Gouda	Warris, J.	Noltee, C.J. (Cees)	Mensink.	
							Boerma geb. Buurman (v), J.M.A. Zaandam	de Jongh, drs. A.H. Leerdam	van der Steen, H. 's-Hertogenbosch	Ringnalda, B. (Bouwe)			
							Kamsteeg, A.T. Dordrecht	de Jonge,	Kossen, P. Groot				

142 Provincial and Federal Governments: Building Your Knowledge

FPTP-PR System

Some countries, like Germany and New Zealand, have developed "hybrid" systems with a combination of the two systems, called FPTP-PR. In Germany, voters cast two votes, one for a representative in their riding and one for the party of their choice. Half the members of the German Parliament come from the riding votes and the other half from the Party votes.

Infosource 4–25 ▼

FPTP AND FPTP-PR COMPARED

This table compares results for Ontario's 1999 provincial election.

	Liberals	NDP	PC
Actual (FPTP):	35	9	59
If FPTP-PR had been used:	38	12	53

One of the advantages of Canada's FPTP system is its simplicity.

Preferential Ballot System

The preferential ballot system is another possibility. In this system, which is used in Australia, citizens vote once, listing their top three choices of candidates. After officials count the first place votes, if the votes for the leading candidate represent less than 50 per cent of the voters, they count the second and third place votes. This system ensures that the winner receives a majority of the votes.

HOW THE PREFERENTIAL BALLOT SYSTEM WORKS

Imagine that in an election people listed their top three choices of candidates, instead of only one. A completed ballot might look like this:

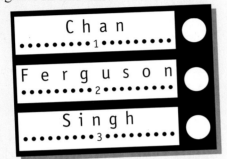

After officials count all the first-place votes, the tally for this constituency is:

Chan	6 000
Ferguson	10 000
Singh	9 000

In a first past the post system, Ferguson would be elected with 40 per cent of the votes (10 000 out of 25 000). In a preferential system, the ballots of Chan, who finished in third place, would be re-examined. These votes would be divided up between Ferguson and Singh, depending on who received second-place support in these ballots. The second-place choice on these ballots would be counted. If Singh received 5000 of these votes, and Ferguson received 1000, the new tally would be:

Ferguson	11 000
Singh	14 000

Now Singh would have the support of 56 per cent of the votes in the riding and would be elected.

ANALYZING THE ISSUE

BE Informed

1. a) In your own words, state the issue discussed in this section.
    b) What criticism of our electoral system is provided in Infosource 4–23?
    c) What argument is provided in Infosource 4–24 to support our electoral system?

2. PR, FPTP-PR, and the preferential ballot are alternatives to our current electoral system. Make a chart that shows the advantages and disadvantages of each option.

3. Which of the electoral systems, including FPTP, do you think is most fair? Give three reasons to support your view.

4. Do you think Canada should change its FPTP system? Why or why not?

5. Visit the Elections Canada Web site to find out about proposed changes to our electoral system. Report on your findings.

BE Informed

1. Use each of the following terms in a sentence, taking care to show how the term is connected to citizenship at the provincial or federal level.
   a) prime minister
   b) legislative branch
   c) member of Parliament
   d) judicial branch
   e) responsible government
   f) party platform

2. With a partner, prepare a mind map that shows how government decisions are made at the federal level. Include the following:
   - Which factors make governments act
   - How government representatives are selected
   - How government is organized to make decisions
   - What role political parties play
   - How citizens participate

   In your mind map, use colours, words, arrows, symbols, and other visuals to highlight key points.

3. Work in a group of three. Over the course of a week, find out what issues are currently being raised by the Opposition. One student should gather information by watching question period on the parliamentary channel C-Pac (Canadian Public Affairs Channel) or current event shows on TVO; the second student should monitor newspapers; the third student should watch television news. Each student should record his or her observations and share findings with the group.
   - What issues are being raised by the Opposition?
   - What is the style and tone of question period?
   - Why do you think some issues are receiving more attention than others?
   - In what way is the Opposition trying to keep the government accountable?

BE Purposeful

4. a) Find out the major provincial party's positions on the following issues. Call the party offices or your MPP to get information. Make a chart of your findings.
   - environment
   - funding for special education
   - hospital services
   - taxation

   b) Prepare a position paper outlining your views on one of these issues. This will require further research. Send your position paper to the relevant cabinet minister and the Opposition critic.

5. Imagine that an MP believes there should be no limits on the right to smoke. Her party, however, wants to ban the sale of tobacco products in drugstores and food stores, to cut down on opportunities for young people to buy cigarettes. The MP surveys her constituents and finds that 64 per cent of them support banning tobacco altogether. What would you advise the MP to do? Discuss your views with the class.

BE Active

6. Choose a current provincial issue that interests you.
   a) Read about this issue in newspapers and magazines.
   b) Imagine that you work in the provincial department that is drafting laws in this area. You have been asked by cabinet to draft a bill that would respond to current concerns. With a partner, prepare a bill that begins with "Be it resolved...." Write a complete paragraph to make the intentions of your bill clear. Your bill should:
   - state who or which groups are expected to obey it
   - state what the penalty will be for those who disobey it
   - be enforceable
   - be in keeping with the values of society
   - not conflict with existing laws
   - be fair
   - be clearly worded, and clear in meaning

   c) Present your bill to other students in a small group. Review the bill, using the points above as a guide.
   d) Write a second draft of your bill, and present it to the class. Incorporate any changes suggested by the class.
   e) Create a scroll on which you write your final draft for display in the class.

CHAPTER 5

Provincial and Federal Governments: Investigating the Issues

FOCUS YOUR LEARNING

The Informed Citizen

What are the processes that protect and strengthen our rights and responsibilities?

How are government structures and processes changing in order to strengthen our democratic traditions?

The Purposeful Citizen

Is it a citizen's responsibility to ensure that his or her rights are protected?

The Active Citizen

How can groups and individuals safeguard their rights and responsibilities?

What actions can you take to ensure governments support your right to be heard?

In Chapter 4, we examined our provincial and federal governments and their powers to govern the country. But how can we ensure that members of the government — once they are elected — do not abuse their powers? In the democratic tradition, people must be able to voice their opinions and continue to influence government, even after elections.

In this chapter, you will look at the processes that safeguard, or protect, our democratic tradition. You will also see ways in which our democratic tradition is changing — evolving as it adapts to changes in Canadian society. You will explore the roles of governments, groups, and individuals in transforming Canada's democratic tradition. You will consider the part that you, too, can play.

Key Terms

- equality rights
- mass media
- pressure group
- lobbying
- lobbyist
- protest group
- civil disobedience

WHAT DO YOU THINK?

In the early 1990s, several terrible crimes involving guns made headlines. Groups and individuals throughout the country began pushing for tighter gun control laws. In response, the federal government passed Bill C-68, which required all gun owners to register their firearms. Some groups, however, opposed the government measures. Aboriginal groups and hunters, in particular, felt the new laws were unfair to them. They felt the legislation would affect law-abiding citizens, rather than criminals.

The government had tried to act to protect the common goals of society, by cutting down on crime, but the result was disagreement among groups on both sides of the issue.

- What different points of view on gun control are presented in the photographs above?

- Why did the federal government decide that stricter gun control was needed? Do you agree or disagree with the government's decision? Give reasons for your view.

- Governments often try to balance the common interests of society with the rights of individuals, but the result is often conflict. In your view, should the common goals of society be emphasized over the rights of individuals? Should the rights of individuals be protected? Explain.

How Is Our Government Changing?

As you saw in Chapter 1, a true democracy is a system in which decisions are made by the people and for the people. In Canada we have government structures and processes that allow decisions to be made in a democratic manner. There are also processes that allow the way we are governed to change. The different branches of our provincial and federal governments continue to evolve so that we can safeguard our democratic traditions and improve on them.

Let us start by looking at changes in the judicial branch.

The Charter and a Changing Role for the Judicial Branch

As you saw in Chapter 2, the Charter of Rights and Freedoms became part of Canada's constitution in 1982. The Charter brought a fundamental change to the ways in which Canadians think about their rights and how they are governed. With some limitations, the Charter stated that all Canadians enjoy certain rights and freedoms. It also gave the judicial branch of government more influence. More and more, the courts have been called on to make judgments about government laws in light of the Charter. Before the Charter, the decisions of Parliament carried the most influence. After 1982, every action of Parliament was subject to the Charter. The courts gained more power, especially the Supreme Court of Canada.

Until 1982, Canadian citizens were rarely able to challenge the law. Since then, people who believe their Charter rights are being infringed by a law have the opportunity to challenge that law in court. For this reason, too, the courts have much more power now than they did before 1982. Many laws and lower-court rulings have been appealed to the Supreme Court of Canada, on the grounds that they go against rights that are protected by the Charter.

Supreme Court Chief Justice Beverley McLachlin. She is the first female Supreme Court chief justice in Canada.

The Supreme Court has been especially active in defining **equality rights** that are protected by the Charter. One of the most famous of these cases was that of Justine Blainey. The Ontario Hockey Association said she could not play hockey on a boys' team. She fought this decision all the way to the Supreme Court, and won her case. The Ontario Human Rights Code, which until then permitted sexual discrimination in amateur sport, was changed.

Some Supreme Court decisions on Charter cases have been very controversial. In 1995, for example, the Supreme Court struck down the Products Control Act, which banned tobacco advertising. The court ruled that the Act infringed on the tobacco industry's right to free expression, a right guaranteed by the Charter. In the opinion of the justices, the Canadian government had failed to show that a total ban on advertising was necessary to protect Canadians' health.

In other cases, the Supreme Court has allowed laws that restricted freedoms, despite Charter guarantees, but only for the good of society. Under the Charter, Canadians have a basic right to "freedom of association" (that is, the right to choose their companions). During the 1990s, biker gangs in Montreal were involved in a series of violent deaths and acts of destruction. In response, Parliament passed the Anti-gang Measures Act, which banned gatherings of individuals identified as members of criminal gangs. The bill restricted freedom of association, but the aim was to decrease organized crime. When the law was challenged, the Supreme Court ruled that it was a "reasonable limit prescribed by law as can be justified in a free and democratic society."

equality rights: Rights, guaranteed in the Canadian Charter of Rights and Freedoms, forbidding discrimination based on the following grounds: age, colour, family status, mental or physical ability, national or ethnic origin, pardoned convictions, religion, or sex.

Bikers ride away from the Ontario legislature after protesting against what they feel is unfair treatment of bikers by all levels of government.

The Charter has changed the ways in which we think about our rights and the way in which we are governed. But does the judicial branch now have too much power? Do Canadians need a further safeguard? Infosource 5–1 gives one point of view.

Infosource 5–1 ▼

QUESTIONING THE NEW ROLE OF THE SUPREME COURT

The role of the Supreme Court has changed dramatically over the last two decades with the introduction of the Canadian Charter of Rights and Freedoms. Supreme Court justices now make decisions that affect our daily lives. Yet their judicial philosophy remains completely unknown to most Canadians before they are appointed. This is because Supreme Court justices are never subject to any kind of public questioning, be it before a parliamentary committee or elsewhere. Of course, prime ministers have not been keen to dilute in any way their absolute power to appoint judges. And possible appointees do not relish the idea of being grilled by a parliamentary committee. But in the end, there is something completely undemocratic in the way these justices are appointed.

Source: Printed in Edmonton Sun

ACTIVITIES   THE INQUIRING CITIZEN

BE Informed

1. State two ways in which the Charter influences the rights and freedoms of Canadians.

2. In what ways has the Charter changed the role of courts in Canada? Provide evidence to support your answer.

3. a) Compare the Supreme Court decisions on the Products Control Act and the Anti-gang Measures Act.
   b) Do you think these decisions were made "by the people and for the people"? Explain.

BE Purposeful

4. a) According to Infosource 5–1, how has the role of the Supreme Court changed? What is the author's view of this changing role?
   b) Do you agree or disagree with the author? What steps would you recommend to resolve the author's concerns?

5. What impact do you think the Charter has had on democratic traditions in Canada?

Should Schools Have the Right to Search Students?

Sometimes our laws appear to be contradictory. For example, the Charter of Rights and Freedoms guarantees the right of all Canadians to be free from unreasonable search and seizure. At the same time, the Education Act says that it is the duty of a principal to "maintain proper order and discipline in the school." The Young Offenders Act states that young people have the right to be heard in the courts and to participate in the processes that lead to decisions that affect them. It also states that young persons should have special guarantees of their rights and freedoms.

The Case of R. v. M.R.M.

All of these legal issues played a part in the court case of a 13-year-old student at a junior high school in Nova Scotia in 1998. During the case, the student was identified as "M.R.M." His initials were used because the Young Offenders Act states that an accused person under the age of 18 cannot be named in public.

The vice-principal of the school had been told by several students that M.R.M. was selling drugs on school property. The students said that M.R.M. would most likely be selling drugs at an upcoming school dance. The vice-principal believed the information was true. The students knew M.R.M. well, and they had provided reliable information in the past.

Schools have been challenged for searching student lockers. The courts have upheld the right of schools to examine lockers when students had prior notice of the search. Courts have stated that searches should be based on a reasonable suspicion that specific illegal items might be found.

That evening, when M.R.M. arrived at the dance, the vice-principal called the police. The vice-principal asked M.R.M. and his friends to accompany him to his office, and then asked the students if they had any illegal drugs. He warned them that he was going to search them. A police officer observed the interview. The vice-principal asked M.R.M. to turn out his pockets and roll up his pants. The vice-principal then found a small bag in M.R.M.'s sock. He handed the bag to the police officer, who confirmed that the bag contained marijuana. The police officer, who had not spoken during the search, now told M.R.M. that he was under arrest, and would be charged for possession of a narcotic. He also told M.R.M. that he had the right to a lawyer and the right to call his parents.

The case went to trial at the Nova Scotia provincial court. The judge ruled that the evidence (the marijuana) had been gathered in a manner that contravened M.R.M.'s Charter right to protection from unreasonable search and seizure. The judge found that the vice-principal was acting as an agent of the police when he conducted the search, and no search warrant had been obtained. Since there was no other evidence, the charge was dropped.

The case was appealed by the Crown (the government prosecutor). The Nova Scotia Court of Appeal overturned the ruling of the judge in the first trial. M.R.M. then appealed this second ruling, and the case went to the Supreme Court of Canada.

These students were searched after some area schools received a bomb threat. According to the guidelines in Infosource 5–2, was the search justifiable?

The Supreme Court stated that schools have special and important duties, and that they must have flexibility in addressing discipline problems. This flexibility includes the right to search a student "where that student is reasonably suspected of being in possession of a prohibited weapon or an illicit drug." The court laid out some general guidelines for school searches, including those shown in Infosource 5–2.

In the final analysis, the court decided to dismiss M.R.M.'s appeal. The court felt the vice-principal did have reasonable grounds to believe that there had been a breach of school rules prior to the search.

Infosource 5–2 ▼

GUIDELINES FOR SCHOOL SEARCHES

- A school does not need a warrant to search a student.

- The school must have reasonable grounds to believe the search will reveal evidence of wrong-doing.

- Reasonable grounds include information received from one student considered to be credible; information received from more than one student; and the observations of a teacher or principal.

- The nature of the information must be compelling and credible, as assessed by the school in the context of the circumstances at that particular school.

ANALYZING THE ISSUE

BE Informed

1. What was the main issue in the case of R. v. M.R.M.?

2. What were the arguments in defence of M.R.M.? What were the arguments against him?

3. What was the final outcome of the case? What legal principles guided the final judgment?

BE Purposeful

4. Do you think the Charter improved the rights of M.R.M. in this case? Provide evidence to support your view.

BE Active

5. a) Investigate the work of the Canadian Youth Rights Association (CYRA) at www.cyra.org. What does CYRA do?

   b) Research one of the current issues with which it is concerned. Possibilities include voting age, schools, media, age discrimination, and curfews. Prepare a short report of your findings. Describe the issue, the conflicting opinions, the role of the Charter, and what young people are doing to bring about change to what they see as injustice.

A Changing Role for the Senate

The legislative branch, like the judicial branch, is evolving. In recent years, the Senate has been the focus of attention.

The Senate provides "sober second thought" to all legislation passed by the House of Commons. In this way, it acts as a check on the power of the governing party. The Senate has the power to reject bills or to recommend changes to bills still under debate. No bill can become law unless it has been passed by the Senate.

In reality, the Senate rarely exercises its power to reject bills, but it can delay their passage until a session of Parliament ends. The delay will then keep a bill from becoming law until further debate. The Senate can also insist that the Commons accept its proposed amendments, which might be more in keeping with citizens' views. The two Houses often reach a compromise. One example was the case of the GST. This tax was introduced in 1990, with many complaints from the public. The Senate failed to defeat the bill that brought the tax in, but it did succeed in reducing the tax from 9 per cent to 7 per cent.

It is the job of senators to be well informed about public issues, so that they can represent the public. They work on various committees and task forces that examine difficult issues. Members of the Senate may also initiate bills. These bills are then debated and passed by the Senate before they are presented to the House of Commons. In this case, the House of Commons is the safeguard.

The Senate chamber, in Ottawa

Suggestions for Senate Reform

Some Canadians believe that it is time for the Senate to be reformed, to protect the rights of all Canadians better. You saw in Chapter 4 that senators are appointed, not elected. Some Canadians believe it is not democratic for people who are not elected to hold so much power. Because senators are appointed by the prime minister, they often represent the same party platform. Therefore, they are likely to approve the bills put forth by the party in the House of Commons. In 2000, the Liberals were the governing party. Infosource 5–3 shows how they dominated the Senate, as well.

Some critics also say that the appointed Senate does not represent Canada's regions fairly. They point out that provinces with bigger populations have many more Senate seats than the smaller ones. The provinces with smaller populations have few senators to speak for their interests, and feel under-represented.

Still other critics argue that senators are not responsible to the people. Even senators who appear not to be doing much work continue to hold their positions. All of these critics seek Senate

Infosource 5–3 ▼

PARTY STANDINGS IN THE SENATE, 2000

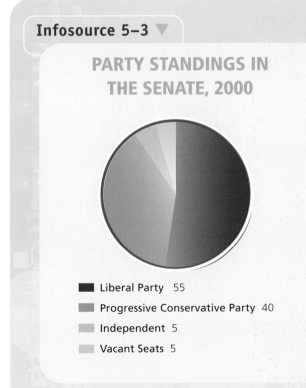

- ■ Liberal Party 55
- ■ Progressive Conservative Party 40
- ■ Independent 5
- ■ Vacant Seats 5

Infosource 5–4 ▼

PROVINCIAL AND REGIONAL REPRESENTATION IN THE SENATE, 2000

Provinces	Seats
Ontario and Quebec	24 each
Nova Scotia and New Brunswick	10 each
British Columbia, Alberta, Saskatchewan, Manitoba, and Newfoundland	6 each
Prince Edward Island	4 seats
Nunavut, Yukon, and Northwest Territories	1 each

Did You Know?

Some people say that an equal number of senators from each province would not be democratic, given the unequal numbers of people in each province.

reform — changes that will make the Senate more responsible to the people. The proposed changes are referred to as a Triple-E Senate (elected, equal, effective):

- Senators should be *elected*.
- Each province of Canada should be represented *equally* in the Senate.
- The revised Senate would be more active in monitoring the actions of the national government, becoming more *effective*.

Here are some differing opinions on both sides of the issue.

Infosource 5–5 ▼

The Senate Should Be Appointed

An elected Upper House would naturally end up challenging the House of Commons. In our system, it is the Commons that determines key elements of government and social policy. The present Senate regularly improves legislation so that it does what it was meant to do, to safeguard minority or general human rights. However, although it has wide powers under the Constitution, the Senate rarely defeats a basic policy the government has approved. Australia's experience suggests that an elected Senate holding these same powers might not be so scrupulous.

Source: Senator Joan Fraser, National Post

Infosource 5–6 ▼

Better Minority Representation in an Appointed Senate

Why should non-elected people have a position of such authority in a democracy? One answer is that Canadians who would not normally become politicians can find their way into the Senate. An example is Thelma Chalifoux, a 68-year-old Métis activist from Alberta. Chalifoux promises to press both women's and Aboriginal issues in the Canadian Senate. Chalifoux says that she would never have gotten into the Senate if the Senate were elected. The reason is simple: she doesn't have the money to run a successful election campaign. "If it was elected, I never would have had a chance. I'm a woman, I'm Métis, and I don't have the finances."

Source: London Free Press

The Senate Should Be Elected

Alberta was the first province to enact legislation embracing the concept of a Triple-E Senate. Alberta's two elected senators — myself and Ted Morton — were given a larger number of votes for seats in Parliament than anyone in the history of Canada. Alberta proved conclusively that Canadians would vote for senators when they have a chance. The road to Senate reform has passed through the government of Alberta. In national polls, support for it outnumbers the membership in all political parties put together.

Source: Senator Bert Brown, Calgary Sun

Whose point of view does this cartoon represent? What does this cartoon say about provincial representation in the Senate?

ACTIVITIES   THE INQUIRING CITIZEN

BE Informed

1. In what ways does the Senate safeguard democratic traditions? In what ways might it be seen as blocking democracy in Canada?

2. List the suggestions that have been made to strengthen the democratic nature of the Senate.

BE Purposeful

3. a) Make a two-column chart listing arguments for appointing the Senate and arguments for electing the Senate.

   b) Within each column, rank the arguments from most to least persuasive.

   c) Can you now form an opinion about whether the Senate should be appointed or elected? If so, what is it? If not, what further information do you feel you need? Discuss your views with the class.

   d) What impact do you think changes to the Senate would have on our democratic traditions?

What Is the Role of the Media?

The **mass media** can be active critics of government. If the government acts unwisely, or if government officials are corrupt, the media draw the public's attention to these problems. The media report on the successes and mistakes of the government. In Canada, newspaper and magazine editorials, television and radio public affairs programs are free to criticize government actions and to question the decisions made by elected representatives. In this way, the media can be a strong safeguard for democratic ideals.

The media also act as outlets for public opinion. You can make your views known by writing a letter to the editor of your local newspaper. Or you can call an open line talk show on your local radio station, be interviewed by a reporter, or even submit a videotape of your comments to a local community cable broadcast. Through the media, citizens can participate in public debates.

The media are also the primary source of information by which citizens form their opinions. For example, it was through the media that the Canadian public was first made aware of the dangers of acid rain. When a bill is proposed in Parliament, newspapers and television reports inform the public about the content of the legislation. Citizens can better understand — and therefore better influence — government decision making because of the information provided by the media.

What does this cartoon say about the media and the general public's attention span? Do you agree?

Calvin and Hobbes   by Bill Watterson

Concerns About Media Influence

The media serve as a go-between, providing Canadians with insights into the politics of our nation. Issues that receive large amounts of media coverage will probably get more attention from the public — and therefore from the government — than issues ignored by the media. The media often focus on what makes a good story, rather than on what makes responsible government policy or action. Too often, the media strive for sensationalism to hold the public interest and sell their papers or their television programming.

In addition, media ownership today is in the hands of only a handful of large publishers. Because publishers and the news editors they employ have so much power over public opinion, this is becoming an issue of concern. In 1989, there were 119 daily newspapers in Canada. Of those, only 23 were independently owned, while 96 were owned by large corporations. Ten years later, the number of dailies had fallen to 106, with one chain, Hollinger Inc./Southam Inc., holding 60 — more than half of the total. Only seven newspapers were independently owned. As a result, the media represent a fairly narrow range of opinions.

Though the media can act as an important safeguard for citizens, they must also be closely examined. Gathering information from the media often requires the reader or viewer to decide what is important, what is factual, and what is biased. Responsible readership — the need to evaluate what you are reading — has become even more relevant with the new technology. With the emergence of online magazines, sites for news and politics, and chat rooms, the Internet is now a major source for information.

One way citizens can use the media to voice their opinions is to appear on "Speaker's Corner," a video booth that records citizens' opinions and later airs them on the local television station. There are variations of Speaker's Corners all around the world.

All the News That's Fit to Filter

A few years ago, reporters at an established newspaper crowded into a conference room to meet their new publisher…. The publisher, one of a new breed of executives who do not require experience in an industry to become a captain of it, had been hired to run the newspaper because of his outstanding record as a "profit maximizer" in the food industry.

"How do you read a newspaper?" asked one reporter.

"Well, I go to the business section first," he said. "Then if I have the time, the sports scores."

"Do you read the editorials?" asked the nervous reporter. "News? Letters to the editor?"

The publisher waved his hand. "Non-essential information," he said.

Reporters predicted an early demise for this publisher. He was, in fact, gone within the year, but for reasons unrelated to his unsettling reading habits. The joke, however, was on the reporters, because the publisher had given them a glimpse of the future. That future is called "customized news" or, more accurately, news filters. The Internet is allowing readers to become their own publishers, filtering the news they get according to their personal interests…. Newspapers — reputable ones at least — try to provide a product that will turn their readers into reasonably well-informed people. Online filters won't do that.

Source: Globe and Mail

ACTIVITIES   THE INQUIRING CITIZEN

BE Informed

1. **a)** Examine the front page of
    [M] two national newspapers on the
    same day. What are the main issues reported? In what ways are
    they similar and different? What
    do you think accounts for the
    similarities and differences?
    b) What should be the qualities
    of a news source on provincial or
    national issues?

BE Active

2. Arrange a tour of a radio or TV
    [M] station. Prepare questions to find
    out how the station develops
    and reports its news stories.

3. Prepare a proposal for a public
    affairs program that focuses on
    civic issues of interest to teens.
    Outline the target audience,
    typical stories, and qualities
    required of the host.

Resolving Conflicts

Whether you belong to the youth group of a political party or to any other group, you will sometimes have to deal with differences of opinion. How can such conflicts be resolved? The following guide can be useful.

Step 1 Define the problem.

Step 2 Understand both sides of the conflict.

Step 3 Identify and assess different solutions.

Step 4 Search for an acceptable compromise.

Sometimes an outside person, or third party, can help find a compromise. This third party might be a **mediator** (someone who helps the two sides to negotiate with each other) or an **arbitrator** (someone who settles the dispute with his or her own solution). The third party has a large responsibility: to find a solution to which both parties will agree, in a process that seems fair to all. If you are asked to find a solution for two other parties, here are some key points:

- Decide what interests lie behind the position of each side.

- Help each side realize what their real interests are.

- Get each side to see the other's point of view and find some common ground in the two positions.

- Involve both parties as much as you can.

- Make sure you are able to justify your position.

Putting It Into Practice

1. Identify a conflict you have recently experienced or witnessed. Was the conflict resolved? If so, how? Were the steps above used to resolve the conflict? Explain. Might the conflict have been resolved more successfully? If so, how?

2. In what situations might it be a good idea for a third party to get involved? Give some characteristics that would be helpful for a third party trying to find a solution to a conflict.

What Are Pressure Groups and Lobby Groups?

How can citizens work together to voice their opinions and influence the government decision-making process? As you saw in Chapter 3, there is strength in numbers. Organizing as a group allows citizens more access to politicians. A large group of like-minded citizens can mount an effective campaign that might eventually persuade politicians to support their cause. Most of the time, the larger the group, the better the results.

A **pressure group**, as the name suggests, is an organized group of people working together to "pressure" or persuade decision makers to promote their common interests. Their final goal is often to change government policy, as they see fit. Pressure groups include organizations whose interests are:

- primarily economic
- religious
- medical and health-related
- concerned with issues of equality
- environmental

pressure group: An organized group of individuals with common interests and concerns who attempt to influence decision makers.

What types of issues is each of these pressure groups primarily concerned with?

CONSUMERS' ASSOCIATION OF CANADA
L'ASSOCIATION DES CONSOMMATEURS DU CANADA

GREENPEACE

THE COUNCIL OF CANADIANS / LE CONSEIL DES CANADIENS

CANADIAN CANCER SOCIETY / SOCIÉTÉ CANADIENNE DU CANCER

Canadian Council of Christians and Jews
Conseil Canadien des Chrétiens et des Juifs

When pressure groups become highly organized, they are sometimes called lobby groups. **Lobbying**, a major pressure group activity, is an attempt to influence decision makers in an organized manner, for example, by one-on-one meetings or phone or letter-writing campaigns. The group may also take its message to the public in an attempt to gain support for its views and increase pressure on decision makers.

Pressure and lobby groups have, over the years, persuaded governments to write new legislation, move airports and industries, establish parks and wildlife reserves, reduce taxes for certain industries, control pollution, and provide more government funding for research and development of certain products and services.

lobbying: Attempts to influence decision makers through direct persuasion, discussion, or persistent attention.

Pressure groups sometimes campaign with posters. What is the point made by this poster?

Infosource 5–9 ▼

Activities of Lobby Groups

Lobby groups communicate their message to government in similar ways. They may:

- organize letter-writing campaigns, collect signatures on petitions, or hold public rallies or protests

- use advertising campaigns on radio, television, and in newspapers to make the public aware of the group's message

- use their membership list to impress upon government officials the widespread support for the group's goals, as well as the importance of prominent group members

- hire lawyers and try to use existing laws to start or stop government action

- raise funds to carry out their activities

Nrinder Nindy Kaur Nann

National Representative on
Youth Issues with the Canadian
Labour Congress (CLC)

Nrinder Nindy Kaur Nann, age 23, is a full-
time employee with the Canadian Labour
Congress, the lobby group which represents
2.3 million unionized workers throughout
Canada. Here are some of her thoughts about
her job and her organization.

**Q: What is your role in the Canadian
Labour Congress?**
A: My job is to represent young people's issues
to the Canadian labour movement and, in turn,
to represent the Canadian labour movement to
the youth population of Canada. I am the only
young person employed by the CLC. But
within our structure we have a CLC youth committee that is made up of representatives from
various unions across Canada — all under the
age of 26. We meet up to four times a year to
set a national agenda for young people.

**Q: What projects have you worked on
recently?**
A: On September 5th, to celebrate Labour
Day, we hosted a five-hour outdoor youth
festival. We had DJs, local artists, rappers, and
singers perform on the main stage,
highlighting their talents as young employable
people. As a labour movement, we were
saying, "Hey, we already know you work, and
we know that you work one, two, or three jobs
to pay off your tuition. So why don't you join
us and celebrate yourselves." We dubbed the
event: "This is no longer your father's labour
movement."

**Q: How do labour issues affect young
people today?**
A: Disrespect is the number one issue that
young people face in the workplace. Whether
in a part-time job at McDonald's, or in retail,
wholesale, or contract jobs, young people are
expected to churn out production at a rate
that's pretty insane. And at the end of the day,
they aren't respected for their work. Often,
they're ridiculed in front of customers or bad-
mouthed in front of co-workers.

Another issue is disregard for the Basic
Employment Standards Act, which states the
minimum rights that an employer is required by
law to provide. When it comes to young people,
these rights are often compromised. Even
though they are adult enough to be officially
employed, young people still don't know their
own rights in the workplace. This education is
not available in the public school system. That's
where we at the CLC come in: number one, we
lobby the government; number two, we provide
this education wherever we can.

Some pressure groups, such as the Canadian Labour Congress, have been in existence for decades. Other groups spring up in response to a particular event. These groups, focusing on a single issue, are more common at the local level. For example, a group of parents in your neighbourhood may wish to have a traffic light installed to allow their children to cross a busy street more safely. Such a group is held together by one specific goal. It usually disbands once the goal is achieved.

The Role of the Professional Lobbyist

The money collected by a pressure group may be used to hire staff or to open offices in Ottawa and provincial capitals. Pressure groups that have the funds often hire people called **lobbyists**. Lobbyists specialize in dealing with government representatives in an attempt to influence public policy. Often experts in the field, they may also provide the group with research and other information that supports the interest group's position. This includes opinion polls or studies of the benefits and costs of a particular policy. They provide the government with clear and quick information that can be used in making decisions. A group in a position to provide constant information to the government may influence government decisions with its input.

lobbyist: A person who is hired to represent the interests of a group by influencing decision makers in the group's favour.

Critics argue that if the government is influenced by lobbyists — who represent minority interests — then the wishes of the unorganized majority may not be heard. A major difference also exists between the influence of well-funded professional lobbyists — for example, those who work for wealthy corporate pressure groups — and those who act on behalf of smaller non-profit organizations. Is it in the public interest for well-funded pressure groups, who can afford to employ expensive lobbyists, to lobby politicians? Critics express concern that such influence can backfire. Rather than being a safeguard, lobbyists might become a threat to democracy.

A lobby group in Nova Scotia protests cuts to government programs that assist people with disabilities.

Questioning the Ethics of Lobbyists

Why should Canadians be concerned about the rise of lobbying? Because lobbying straddles the very distinction between the public and private spheres of Canadian society. For money, lobbyists represent or assist private interests in their efforts to influence public life. Where does private interest end and public interest begin when it comes to lobbying?

This problem is most evident...where high-profile lobbyists-for-profit are the same people actively working at the highest levels of our national political parties. These lobbyist activists are in a position to mingle their public activities in political parties with the private interests they represent for pay.

Source: Toronto Star

ACTIVITIES   THE INQUIRING CITIZEN

BE Informed

1. a) Explain, in your own words, the meaning of the terms "pressure group" and "lobby group."
b) Identify different actions these groups take to achieve their goals.

2. a) What is a lobbyist?
b) What does Nrinder Nindy Kaur Nann's work as a lobbyist involve?

BE Purposeful

3. a) In what ways does Nrinder Nindy Kaur Nann's work help to safeguard the rights of young people?
b) In what ways might lobbying hinder our democratic processes?

BE Active

4. a) Select one of the provincial or national pressure groups mentioned in this section, and find out more about it. The group's Web site is a good place to start your research.
b) Investigate the group's history and membership, and describe in detail one example of how this group attempted to put pressure on the government, and for what purpose. What influence did the group have on the government's decision?
c) To what extent do you think its action acted as a safeguard or threat to democratic decision making?

The Case of the Tobacco Industry: Do Lobby Groups Work for the Common Goals of the People?

During the 1990s, the Canadian government struggled to devise a law that would put strict controls on tobacco packaging, advertising, and sales — and still be fair to different interest groups. The most controversial issue became whether to ban the display of tobacco company names and logos at sports and cultural events they sponsored. Pressure groups on both sides of the issue vigorously lobbied the government.

On one side, anti-smoking pressure groups, such as the Non-Smokers' Rights Association and Physicians for a Smoke-Free Canada, argued that a total advertising ban was essential to keep young people from taking up smoking. On the other side, lobbyists for the Canadian Tobacco Manufacturers' Council argued that advertising was only intended to encourage smokers to change brands, not to attract new smokers. The industry opposed any legislation that would limit their right to advertise or display their company names. They were joined by representatives for several Canadian sports and cultural groups, who stated that they could not afford to hold auto races, jazz festivals, and other such events without tobacco company sponsorship. Which interest groups were most concerned about the common goals of society?

Tobacco companies often sponsor sporting events, such as the tennis tournament shown here. Can you think of other events that are sponsored by tobacco companies?

September 1995

Supreme Court strikes down the Tobacco Products Control Act from 1989. The court rules that the act infringed on the tobacco companies' right to free expression under the Charter of Rights and Freedoms.

December 1995

Minister of Health Diane Marleau produces a Blueprint on Tobacco Control, recommending a complete ban on tobacco advertising, as well as on marketing through sponsored events.

December 1996

Bill C-71, the Tobacco Act, introduced in the House of Commons by Health Minister, David Dingwall. This bill allows tobacco advertising in adult-oriented publications. It also allows companies to use their product names and logos (only on-site) at sponsored events directed to adults.

June 1997

Bill C-71 passes into law with two amendments by the House of Commons. One amendment delays imposing any restrictions on sponsorship (such as showing logos on television broadcasts of sponsored events) until October 1, 1998.

November 1997

International motor racing events are exempted from the Tobacco Act.

June 1998

Minister of Health Alan Rock introduces Bill C-42 to amend the Tobacco Act. This act delays restrictions on sponsorship promotion of tobacco products for five years. (At that time, the tobacco industry was lobbying for a 10-year delay and the anti-smoking forces were lobbying for a complete ban.)

Infosource 5–12 ▼

TOBACCO LOBBY ARGUES AGAINST RESTRICTIONS

"Sponsorship," says Marie-Josée Lapointe, Communications Director of the Canadian Tobacco Manufacturers' Council, is a way of "maintaining corporate identity" — not luring new smokers. "If Air Canada sponsors a film festival," she adds, "do you get a sudden urge to buy a plane ticket and take off?"

Source: Maclean's

Infosource 5–13 ▼

THE ANTI-SMOKING POINT OF VIEW

The new proposed amendments to the Tobacco Act [delaying restrictions on cigarette advertising] are a death sentence to young Canadians, says the president of the Canadian Medical Association (CMA).… As long as advertising is restricted, children won't be inspired to start the deadly habit.

Source: Medical Post

Tobacco smoke can harm your children Health Canada

Cigarettes are addictive Health Canada

Smoking can kill you Health Canada

Cigarettes cause strokes and heart disease Health Canada

Do cigarette-box warnings like these counteract the effect of tobacco advertising?

GOOD PUBLIC HEALTH POLICY

Only the naive or wilfully deluded can deny that tobacco sponsorships are simply another form of cigarette advertising, indeed one enormously useful for evading the restriction on advertising to children and young people — the targets for the industry as few people take up smoking over the age of 20. Who goes to the "Symphony of Fire" fireworks? Families with lots of kids. Who goes to the tennis matches, where the ball boys and girls all advertise cigarettes on their T-shirts? How can children and young people not see the massive amount of billboard and sign advertising for all of the jazz, car racing, and music events that ostensibly are announcing a sponsorship, but whose signs and logos all look remarkably like the cigarette package of the company in question?

The cigarette companies do not sponsor arts and sports out of the goodness of their hearts…[they] will fight any restriction that keeps them from getting value for expenditure…. Good public health policy requires an end to all tobacco sponsorships and advertising.

Lynn McDonald, author of the Non-Smokers' Health Act, 1988, former MP, and professor of sociology at the University of Guelph.

Should companies other than tobacco manufacturers be more active in sponsoring sports and cultural events?

The mere whiff of sponsorship restrictions rattles arts and sporting organizations. Among the critics is Ian Allison, vice-president of media affairs and television at Spruce Meadows — the southern Alberta site of the du Maurier Ltd. international show-jumping competition, which boasts a $750 000 top prize donated by Imperial Tobacco. "With ever-reduced public funding, it's one thing to expect excellence from our athletes," says Allison. "But who's going to fund these events, and who's going to make them happen here in Canada?" To the arts — faced with steadily declining government funding — tobacco sponsorships are critical. "These relationships have been with us through thick and thin, unlike government funding," says Kathy Kelly, National Director of the Canadian Conference of the Arts, an Ottawa-based advocacy group.

Source: Maclean's

Why do cigarette companies like du Maurier sponsor events, such as the Montreal Jazz Festival?

ANALYZING THE ISSUE

BE Informed

1. **a)** State the issue in this case.
   b) List the key events that led to the new Tobacco Act.

2. What point of view did anti-smoking groups argue? What point of view did the tobacco lobby argue?

BE Purposeful

3. Work in small groups to role-play a radio interview on this issue. Roles should include the interviewer, a member of an arts or sports group, a member of the Canadian Medical Association, and a member of the Canadian Tobacco Manufacturers' Council. Use the information from the infosources in this section to develop your arguments.

4. **a)** Make a chart showing the three alternative courses of action that were open to the government, and the potential consequences of each one.
   b) Which do you think best represented the common good?

5. **a)** What did the government finally decide to do?
   b) Do you agree or disagree with its decision? Provide evidence to support your view.

Can Individuals Safeguard Democracy?

So far, we have discussed the following safeguards in our democratic system:

- processes within the government itself, such as the court system
- the media, over which citizens have very little control
- pressure or lobby groups, made up of large numbers of people

None of these safeguards is directly in the hands of the average citizen, however. Nor are any of them easy to achieve. Taking an issue to the courts, for example, requires a great deal of time and money. So how can citizens make sure they have a say in the democratic process? Active and responsible citizenship is in itself an important safeguard for democracy. There are many ways to safeguard your rights and to directly or indirectly influence the decision-making process through participation.

Citizens can voice their views within the political process. As a citizen, you have the right to phone, e-mail, or write to your representative or any other politician about a policy or issue that concerns you. At election time, you can voice your approval or disapproval. Party participation and campaign work are other ways of taking a stand and making your views known.

Another safeguard is your ability to voice your views through volunteer work and membership in organizations. You can work for the causes in which you believe. If you are concerned about social justice, volunteer work in your community is a good beginning. Join your local environmental rights group, give money or raise money for your favourite feminist charity, give your time to work at an animal shelter, or start your own school committee that takes action against discrimination in everyday life.

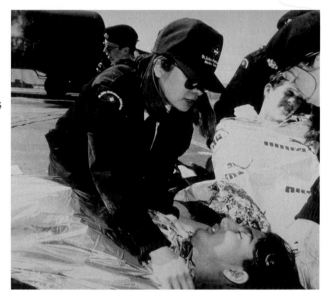

Volunteering with a community service, such as St. John Ambulance, is one way to get involved. Here, volunteers practise their skills during a mock disaster.

Writing Effectively

Whether you are writing a letter to a government official to express your views on an issue or finishing your term assignment, it is important to practise effective writing skills. To **write effectively** means to communicate your ideas directly and clearly.

Here are some suggestions for effective writing.

- **Know your audience.** If you are writing to a friend, your style can be informal. But if you are writing to your government representative, a more formal approach is more appropriate.

- **Research your topic adequately.** The more you know about your topic, the more credibility you will have in your writing.

- **Prepare an outline.** Jot down your main ideas in point form. Organize your arguments from strongest to weakest. Decide if you want to start or end with your strongest point to make your writing most effective. When you have decided on a sequence, begin to write.

- **Use a peer editor.** Have someone review your writing. Ask your editor to check for good communication, as well as for correct grammar and punctuation. Does she or he understand what you are trying to say?

- **Read over your writing at least twice.** Make sure it covers everything you want to say. Check it against your outline.

Putting It Into Practice

1. Read a letter to the editor in your local newspaper. With a partner, assess how well the letter was written, based on the suggestions above.

2. Write a letter to the editor about a current provincial or federal issue that interests you. Follow the guidelines above.

3. As a class, discuss difficulties you had writing the letter. List other guidelines that would help you get your message across more effectively.

Activism and Non-violent Civil Disobedience

Canadians have a reputation for being law-abiding citizens. Yet, if you believe a major injustice is taking place — and traditional methods of voicing your views do not work — how can you let your disapproval of government policies or practices be known? When, if ever, is it acceptable to make a strong stand by violating the law — openly, peacefully, and for a good cause?

Some activists who are concerned with social justice believe that it is sometimes necessary to use more forceful action to achieve their goals. When a group of activists come together at an event they have organized to promote a cause, they become a **protest group**. Political protest groups use direct action such as rallies, parades, marches, sit-ins, public demonstrations, and even road blockades. Their action may include distributing pamphlets, giving public speeches, singing songs and chants of protest, and carrying placards to draw attention to their cause. Environmentalists, for example, might hold a protest rally outside the offices of the industry that is planning to build a new plant. Teachers or nurses may become protestors and join a march on Parliament if they are concerned about legislation that will affect their lives, their work, and their sense of justice.

protest group: A group of individuals who demonstrate together to influence decision makers through direct, sometimes extraordinary, action.

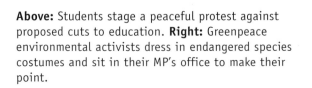

Above: Students stage a peaceful protest against proposed cuts to education. **Right:** Greenpeace environmental activists dress in endangered species costumes and sit in their MP's office to make their point.